GIFTS
FROM THE
GARDEN

100 GORGEOUS HOMEGROWN PRESENTS

GIFTS FROM THE GARDEN

100 GORGEOUS HOMEGROWN PRESENTS

DEBORA ROBERTSON

PHOTOGRAPHY BY YUKI SUGIURA

K

AcKNowLEDGMeNTs

First, I owe enormous gratitude to Kyle Cathie and everyone at Kyle Books for entrusting me with this lovely project. Huge thanks to Judith Hannam for steering me through the initial stages and Sophie Allen whose grace, patience, good humour and razor-sharp mind made this book such a great pleasure to work on. With Helen Bratby, who designed these pages so beautifully, I felt in the safest and most creative of hands.

It is my great good fortune to have had the supremely talented Yuki Sugiura take the photographs for this book. Her enthusiasm for the project made shoot days a delight. And I am enormously indebted to my dear friend, stylist Tabitha Hawkins. I wish we could work together every day.

Thank you to my agent, Caroline Michel at PFD, for her enthusiasm, advice and encouragement. I truly appreciate it.

And an #FF forever to gardening writer and Twitter pal Alex Mitchell, who first suggested I might like to talk to Kyle Books about this project.

Thank you to Nash Khandekar for all of his help and friendship over the years.

My weekly trips to Columbia Road Flower Market are made all the more enjoyable because of Carl, Mick and Sylvia Grover. Their advice, wisdom and friendship have enriched my garden and my Sundays for many years. Long may that continue.

Without my parents' endless patience with a small girl who loved to bake and make and generally leave a crafty mess in her wake, I would never have discovered the love of creating, cooking and growing which continues to add untold pleasure to my daily life. If they're astonished that I somehow managed to spin that into a career, they have the good grace not to show it.

And finally, to my husband Séan, who is the greatest gift I ever gave myself: thank you for your tireless cheerleading, coffee making, clearing up, ferrying around, sampling and suggesting. You're marvellous.

Published in Great Britain in 2012 by
Kyle Books
23 Howland Street
London W1T 4AY
www.kylebooks.com

ISBN: 978-0-85783-081-4

10 9 8 7 6 5 4 3 2 1

Design **Helen Bratby**
Photography **Yuki Sugiura**
Prop styling **Tabitha Hawkins**
Project and food styling **Debora Robertson**
Project editor **Sophie Allen**
Copy editor **Emily Hatchwell**
Proofreader **Ruth Baldwin**
Production **Gemma John and Lisa Pinnell**

A CIP record for this title is available from the British Library.

Colour reproduction by Altaimage
Printed and bound in China by C&C Offset

CONTENTS

INTRODUCTION

Anyone who has ever grown lettuce in a window box or planted some bulbs in an old terracotta pot knows that the pleasure of growing something yourself often far exceeds the effort it takes. And by using the plants you grow to create gifts for those you love, you can share that pleasure and prolong it even further.

Gardeners, like cooks, are generous people. You seldom leave the garden or kitchen of such a person without a cutting, a few seeds, a recipe or a scrap of paper filled with hastily-scrawled tips. Transforming what you grow into gifts takes this instinct, packs it into a jar or box and wraps it all up in a pretty bow. Of course, your intention is to delight the recipient, but there is also a near-addictive enjoyment in creating such gifts too.

Making your own presents enhances your awareness of – and delight in – the passing seasons in unexpected ways. If you've rigged up a simple flower press at home, a country walk or a stroll around the garden is never the same again. You will always have an eye out for interesting leaves or grasses, perfect flowers or seed heads. If you're making your own pot-pourri, every falling petal is no longer a source of sadness – it's an opportunity.

Some gifts, such as a batch of biscuits, a jar of seasoned olives or a simple posy, are the work of a few minutes. Others take a little more forward planning. Chutneys and liqueurs need to mature for a few weeks or months before you give them. But there's something enormously satisfying in knowing that you have a stash of gifts ready to be packed up and given to friends and family.

For some of the gift ideas in this book, there's an initial investment in powders, potions, essential oils and waxes, but a little goes a long way, and lasts a long time. You'll have them on hand next time you want to rustle up a quick bar of soap, face cream or room spray. They'll also allow you to create unique gifts at a fraction of the cost of something mass-produced in a factory.

And there is an added benefit to making your own gifts. Not for you the anxiety-inducing dash along the high street, wearily ticking off gifts from your present list with a resigned 'That'll do.' Making your own gifts allows you to give yourself permission to slow down and spend a few hours, a day or two, in activities which combine both playfulness and usefulness. The intrinsic pleasure in making your own presents means that you'll never have to battle with the crowds in a shopping centre. You also have the comfort of knowing exactly what has gone into your jellies, face masks and polishes – there are no secret or sinister ingredients lurking beneath the pretty lids.

Deciding how to package your presents is almost as much fun as making them. Look out for old tins, pretty jars, lengths of ribbon, tags, stamps and unusual papers and you can wrap them up in a fashion that would rival the attempts of the smartest boutiques.

We all know how much time and love goes into growing your own flowers, fruit, vegetables and herbs. When we transform them into gifts, we're sharing more than a piece of our gardens, we're sharing a piece of our hearts. And there is nothing more generous than that.

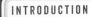

STRAIGHT FROM THE GARDEN

While it's satisfying to create and give presents made from plants you've grown in your garden, sometimes the most touching gift of all is the simplest: a plant you've propagated and tended yourself. It's an inexpensive way of increasing your own stock as well as producing specimens which you can pot up and give to friends.

There's nothing terribly difficult about dividing, layering or taking cuttings to increase your plant supply, so even the most inexperienced of gardeners shouldn't feel daunted about giving it a try.

Taking cuttings

Take softwood cuttings in spring when the plant has plenty of healthy new shoots. Get everything ready before you start. You'll need a pruning knife, a 7cm pot with drainage holes, filled with a mixture of compost and horticultural grit, a watering can with a fine rose, a pencil or dibber, a length of strong wire and a clear plastic bag.

Pull a non-flowering stem, about 10cm long, from the plant with a small strip of bark, or 'heel', attached. Trim the excess off the bark strip with a pruning knife. Use your knife to trim the lower leaves from the stem – you need only a few pairs of leaves to remain at the top and you need a decent length of bare stem to insert into the compost. Make four or five holes around the edge of the pot with a pencil or dibber and insert the prepared stems into them, firming them in gently with your fingers. Water in lightly.

Bend the wire into a loop which clears the tops of the cuttings by several centimetres. Insert the loop into the pot and place the plastic bag over the top, making sure it doesn't touch the leaves.

Put the cuttings in a warm, shaded place and remember to turn the bag inside out every few days to ensure the moisture doesn't drip down onto the leaves and make them wet, as this may cause them to rot. Once rooting is established and the cuttings start to show signs of new growth, snip the corner of the bag to increase circulation.

After 4–6 weeks, remove the bag completely, and when the cuttings start to look like healthy little plants, pot them up individually. Overwinter in a cold greenhouse or conservatory and plant out the following spring.

See page 54 for information on how to take semi-hardwood cuttings.

SoME PLaNTs wHIch YoU cAn pRoPaGaTe bY

TAKING SOFTWOOD CUTTINGS Chamomile, lavender, lemon verbena, pelargoniums, pinks, rosemary, sage

LAYERING Bay, clematis, climbing roses, honeysuckle, pinks, sage, thyme

DIVIDING Bergamot, chamomile, chives, hardy geraniums, lemon balm, lemon grass, mint, pinks, thyme, wormwood

Dividing

Some plants, especially mint, in pots or planted in the ground can die back in the centre or become straggly after a while. Revive congested plants in spring by lifting them with a fork or carefully removing them from their pots. Use a fork, knife or your hands to split the plant into separate pieces, each with their own root system. Replant in pots or in the ground and water in well. When potting up plants, make sure the plant pots you use are scrupulously clean to avoid spreading diseases. Place some broken bits of terracotta pot in the bottom to help drainage and don't fill the pot right up to the brim with soil as this will make it difficult to water your plant later.

If you're using terracotta pots, while they look lovely, you may have a problem with them drying out during hot weather. To avoid this try lining the sides of the pot (don't block up the drainage holes) with plastic. I save empty compost bags and chop them up to line pots with – the tough plastic works very well and doesn't perish.

Layering

This is a very easy way to increase your supply of rosemary and is possibly the simplest propagation method of all.

In summer, choose a long, fresh, flexible, non-flowering stem about 25cm long. Remove the rosemary leaves from all but the top 4–5cm of the sprig and gently roughen the underside of your stem with a pruning knife. This will encourage it to root.

Use a trowel or your fingers to make a thin trench, about 4cm deep, adjacent to the mother plant. Place the prepared stem in the trench, ensuring that the leafy tip remains above the soil level. Make a pin of about 8cm long with a piece of sturdy wire and use this to anchor the stem in the ground. Cover the stem and trench with soil and water in well. Water little and often until the stem shows signs of new growth. In the autumn, if the plant is well rooted, cut it away from its mother plant and pot up. Alternatively, leave it in place until the spring before cutting it away and planting out in a new spot.

HERBS & FLOWERS

Wrapping

A gift looks so much more charming and personal when it's attractively wrapped and embellished with simple cuttings from the garden. Unless you're wrapping and giving the present almost immediately, choose cuttings which will last quite well without wilting, such as evergreen sprigs of bay leaves and rosemary, fir cones or small sprays of berries.

A wintery selection of bay leaves, berries, eucalyptus, fir cones, fir sprigs, holly, ivy, mistletoe, rosemary, dried orange and apple slices (see page 123)

Fine florist's wire
Secateurs
Ribbon, garden string and/or raffia

This is hardly a 'method', more an inspiration. Sprigs or sprays of foliage and herbs can simply be tucked under the ribbon on your parcel, but to make them more secure you can tie them in with wire which will then be hidden by the bow. If you'd like to carry the garden theme even further, garden string and raffia come in many colours and provide an inexpensive, informal and attractive alternative to ribbon.

If you like, berries and holly leaves can be frosted to give them a Christmassy/wintery appearance (see page 121). Fir cones can be sprayed gold, silver or white, which looks particularly effective as an adornment to plain papers.

Growing Bay

Bay, *Laurus nobilis*, is an evergreen member of the laurel family, steeped in ancient folklore. Those handsome bay topiaries you often see outside smart houses? It was believed that planting bay at entry points warded off witches, wizards and lightning. Whether they ward off evil or not, they're enormously useful in the kitchen and not terribly demanding to grow. They're very happy grown in containers, which allows you to bring them inside when hard winter frosts threaten. Water sparingly during the winter and, if you're training your bay into a shape, prune it back in spring to help maintain its structure and promote fresh new growth. Bay trees do best when planted in well-drained soil in a sunny spot where they have some protection from harsh winds, though they will manage a little shade.

Decorative Inspiration

SPRING: Auriculas, fragrant sprigs of *Osmanthus burkwoodii* or *Daphne odora*, variegated *Euonymous fortunei* leaves, ferns, pansies, flowering sprigs of rosemary

SUMMER: Achilleas, astrantias, campanulas, chillies, coneflowers, cornflowers, eryngiums, honeysuckle, some hydrangea blooms, irises, love-in-a-mist, marguerites, marigolds, sprigs of myrtle, pinks, scented pelargonium leaves and flowers, scabious, sunflowers, thrift flowers, roses, salvias, veronica

AUTUMN: Any bright, autumn foliage such as cotinus, *Euonymus alatus*, ginkgo, liquidambar, oak leaves with acorns, maples, asters, Chinese lanterns, dahlias, fennel seed heads, dried honesty seed heads, poppy seed heads, pyracantha berries, rosehips, sorbus berries

Decorated stationery

Pressed flowers, herbs, leaves and seed heads are a great way to decorate gift tags, cards, boxes and name cards for the dinner table, as well as making an original adornment to bought candles (see page 85).

A selection of dried flowers,
    seed heads and/or leaves
A selection of papers
Clear craft glue
Tweezers

SOME GOOD THINGS TO PRESS

Cow parsley or Queen Anne's lace
Delphiniums
Ferns
Forget-me-nots
Single hydrangea blossoms
Larkspur
Pansies
Pinks
Poppies
Primroses
Individual rose petals
Verbena
Violets
Wormwood – flowers and leaves

Pick your specimens in peak condition and choose a dry day, after the morning dew has evaporated. Brush off any dust with a small, soft paintbrush and enclose the flowers in two sheets of blotting paper. Either press them in a heavy book, weighed down beneath other heavy books, or use a flower press (see the box below). They're ready when they're completely dry and papery, which should take a couple of weeks. They're quite fragile, so handle them carefully – you might want to use tweezers.

If you're not using your flowers immediately, seal them in glassine bags and store them in a cardboard box in a cool, dry place.

Cut your papers into the size you want and fold them to make cards. Use a very thin layer of clear craft glue to stick the flowers onto the cards. Less is usually more – a single bloom, a perfect curl of fern, one beautiful leaf can look more elegant and effective than a more elaborate design.

TO MAKE SCENTED STATIONERY

If you're making a box of stationery as a gift, sew a simple muslin sachet (see Herbal Bathtime 'Teas' on page 31) and fill it with dried, scented flower petals and herbs. Tuck the sachet into the gift box and after a week or so it will impart a subtle, sweet scent to the paper.

MAKING YOUR OWN FLOWER PRESS

Of course you can buy a flower press, but often they're small and expensive. If you can drill a hole, they're easy to make yourself. You'll need two pieces of wood: about 30cm square works quite well. In the four corners of each piece drill holes large enough for long bolts to be fitted through them. Cut out squares of cardboard and blotting paper (available from good craft shops, art shops and stationers) small enough to fit the area within the holes. Layer up the cardboard and blotting paper, enclosing the flowers you want to dry between two sheets of blotting paper. Place the bolts through the holes and secure tightly with wing nuts and washers.

tropaeolum majus

...purea

...nthriscus cerefolium

Seed packets

You can be too tidy a gardener. While scrupulously dead-heading plants can prolong flowering, it will deprive you of the pleasure of watching the often beautiful seed heads develop and of the thrifty satisfaction of collecting free seeds. As an added bonus, they make very good gifts for keen gardeners.

Secateurs or scissors
Brown paper bags
Small glassine bags
Labels
Sewing machine or needle and thread

Allow seed heads to dry out as much as possible on the plant. Wait until the seeds look ripe – usually when they've turned brown or black – and choose a dry, still day to harvest them.

Cut off the seed heads, holding a bowl beneath the plant to capture any seeds which may fall as you work. For smaller flowers, such as pansies, it's enough simply to shake the seeds free from the flower heads into a bowl before bagging them up. For larger specimens, place the entire flower head in a paper bag, secure with an elastic band, label and hang upside down in a dry place. When most of the seed pods have opened, tip the bag's contents out onto a pale surface and sort the seeds from any bits of the seed heads.

Put the seeds into the glassine bags and fold down the top. Type or write out seed labels, then secure them by stitching right across the bag. They make good gifts just as they are, but you can also turn them into pretty and unusual gift tags to tie onto presents by simply punching a hole into the seed bag above the line of stitching and threading through string, ribbon or raffia.

Stored in a cool, dry, airy place, seeds will remain viable for years, but germination is more reliable within a year or so.

SOME EASY SEEDS TO COLLECT

Aquilegia
Chives
Chinese lanterns
Foxgloves
Larkspur
Love-in-a-mist
Marigolds
Morning glory
Nasturtiums
Pansies
Poppies
Snapdragons
Sunflowers

Cook's window boxes

A themed window box, tailored to a friend's particular culinary passion, makes an original and thoughtful gift. And, the more you pluck at them, the better they grow.

Pizza window box
1 small rocket plant
1 small basil plant
1 small oregano plant
1 small chilli plant
1 small cherry tomato plant

Thai window box
1 small lemon grass plant
1 small mint plant
1 small coriander plant
1 small Thai basil (*Ocimum basilicum* horapa) and/or Holy basil (*O. sanctum*) plant
1 small chilli plant

Fines herbes window box
1 small chervil plant
1 small tarragon plant
1 small parsley plant
1 small chives plant

Window box, or other suitable container
Broken crocks or pebbles
Compost
Slow-release fertiliser granules

If you're not using a window box, make sure that the container you're using has some drainage holes in the base. Add some broken crocks or pebbles to the bottom and fill with compost mixed with slow-release fertiliser granules, according to the instructions on the packet. Plant up with the chosen herbs and water them in well.

A well-cared-for window box should last all summer.

GROWING ROCKET
Rocket, *Rucola coltivata*, is not only delicious scattered fresh over a just-out-of-the-oven pizza, but it's also great in fiery summer salads and can be whizzed into a sprightly pesto. It's very easy to grow from seed. Sow thinly directly into the ground or pot. It can run to seed quite quickly, so keep cutting at it and ensure it's well watered.

PACKAGING IDEA To make your planter an even more special gift, write out a card with care instructions for the herbs and tie it to the handle of some secateurs or a watering can with a pretty ribbon, garden string or raffia.

Chive & lemon pesto

This is a sprightly, easy pesto to make when you're cutting back the first flush of growth from your chives before they flower. It's delicious on pasta or gnocchi, of course, but it's also very good as a dressing for just-boiled new potatoes. Makes approx. 1 x 190g jar.

40g pine nuts
A generous bunch of chives,
 about 50g, finely chopped
60g Parmesan cheese, finely grated
Grated zest of 1 small lemon
1 small garlic clove, minced
4–6 tablespoons olive oil,
 plus a little more for bottling
Salt and pepper

1 x 190g jar

Warm a dry frying pan over a medium heat and gently toast the pine nuts until just golden and fragrant, rattling the pan frequently to ensure they do not burn. Cool and bash roughly in a pestle and mortar, or pulse a couple of times in a food processor. Combine with the chives, cheese, lemon zest, garlic and just enough oil to get the texture you like. Taste and season if necessary with salt and pepper.

Spoon the pesto into the cold, sterilised jar, pressing down with the back of a spoon to get rid of any air pockets. Ensure that the pesto is completely covered by a thin layer of oil before sealing.

Refrigerated, the pesto will keep for 2–3 days.

GROWING CHIVES

Slender, grassy chives (*Allium schoenoprasum*) are one of the first herbs to poke their way through the soil to herald the beginning of spring. These clump-forming hardy perennials are very easy to grow and have so many uses in the kitchen, they earn their place in even the smallest of gardens. Keep them well watered in dry spells and trim them back quite close to the soil line before flowering to ensure lots of fine leaf growth. If you have room, do allow a clump or two to flower, though. The pretty purple pompoms which appear at the end of the leaves look and taste wonderful in salads.

PACKAGING IDEA To make a more substantial gift, combine this tangy pesto with a bag or two of beautiful fresh pasta and/or a pestle and mortar.

Herbes de Provence

Making your own herbes de Provence allows you to adjust the balance of herbs until you have the flavour you like. Traditionally, this blend is a combination of herbs which grow wild in the hills of the South of France – the lavender is a more modern addition. Makes 1 x 150g jar.

BASIC RECIPE
3 tablespoons dried thyme
2 tablespoons dried marjoram
1 tablespoon dried oregano
1 tablespoon dried summer savory
1 teaspoon dried rosemary
1 teaspoon dried lavender flowers
½ teaspoon fennel seeds
1 dried bay leaf

OTHER ADDITIONS YOU MAY LIKE
A little dried orange or lemon zest
Dried chervil
Dried tarragon
Dried mint
Dried basil
Dried dill

1 storage jar, about 150g capacity

Combine the dried herbs in a pestle and mortar and crush roughly to blend. Seal in your chosen jar, which should be airtight.

This mixture is enormously versatile. It can be used as a dry spice rub for chicken or fish or combined with olive oil to make a marinade, scattered on potatoes before you roast them, sprinkled on pizza, or used to season stuffed tomatoes or in light, summery tomato sauces.

Sealed in an airtight container and stored in a cool, dark place, the herbes de Provence mixture will keep for up to 4 months.

GROWING MARJORAM & OREGANO

Both marjoram and oregano are an invaluable addition to the herb garden, with marjoram having the slightly milder, sweeter flavour which makes it better added towards the end of cooking time. All of the following have excellent flavour: Greek oregano (*Origanum vulgare* subs. *hirtum*), pot marjoram (*O. onites*) and golden marjoram (*O. vulgare* 'Aureum'). Trim the plants after flowering to keep them bushy and cut them back to within about 5cm of the soil line in late autumn.

Seasoned salts

Great for seasoning meat, fish, vegetables and even sprinkling over popcorn, seasoned salts take just seconds to make. Use fresh herbs in the mixture as they have better flavour and will dry out in the salt, infusing it with their aromas. Pack the salts in clear glass jars and give them as a set – their striking colours make for a very attractive gift.

Chilli salt

This salt adds a delicious kick of heat on everything from grilled sardines to steak or roasted potato wedges.

50g sea salt flakes
1 dried chilli
1 teaspoon fresh oregano
½ teaspoon ground cumin
¼ teaspoon smoked paprika

Thyme & orange salt

Very good sprinkled over roasted vegetables.

50g sea salt flakes
Finely grated zest of 1 small orange
2 tablespoons fresh thyme leaves
  and flowers

Citrus salt

Great on white fish, prawns and chicken.

50g sea salt flakes
Finely grated zest of 2 lemons
Finely grated zest of 1 lime

Dill salt

This salt works well sprinkled on salmon or roasted beetroot.

50g sea salt flakes
2 tablespoons fresh dill fronds
Finely grated zest of 1 small lemon
¼ teaspoon freshly ground
  black pepper
A couple of pinches of dill seeds,
  if you have them

To make the seasoned salts, simply pulse the ingredients in a food processor until well blended or pound them together in a pestle and mortar. Store in airtight containers.

The salts will keep their flavours for a couple of months.

Bouquet garni

These little bundles of herbs impart great depth of flavour when added to slowly simmered soups, stews and stocks. But the classic culinary trio of parsley, thyme and bay leaves is really just the starting point. Include some tarragon for chicken or fish, a thinly pared strip of orange zest and some marjoram in bundles intended for beef casseroles, or rosemary to bring flavour to slow-cooked lamb dishes. Bouquet garni bundles make wonderful gifts for friends who are keen cooks.

THE ESSENTIAL COMBINATION

3 parsley stalks
2 thyme sprigs
1 bay leaf

Kitchen string
Labels
Jars

Simply tie together the bundles with string and hang them to dry in a dark, well-ventilated place before storing them in an airtight container. If you are making bundles to go with different kinds of dishes, don't forget to label them.

Stored in an airtight container, the bundles will keep their flavour for a month or so.

To go with chicken

A curl of lemon zest
Sprigs of tarragon
Fennel fronds

To go with beef

A curl of orange zest
Sprigs of marjoram and oregano

To go with pork

A curl of lemon zest
Sprigs of sage and myrtle

To go with lamb

Sprigs of rosemary, oregano
  and marjoram

GROWING DILL

Dill, *Anethum graveolens*, is an annual herb that has an affinity with fish, potato and egg dishes. Either start off the seed in plug trays (it doesn't like its roots disturbed), or sow it directly in the ground. In spring, once all threat of frost has passed, sow the seed thinly and cover with a fine layer of soil. Dill thrives in well-drained, fairly poor soil with a bit of shade. Once the seeds have established themselves, thin to about 25cm apart and water well in hot spells to prevent the plants going to seed. Sow successive plantings over the summer to maintain a continuous supply. In autumn, gather the seeds (see page 19).

COMPANION PLANTING PARSLEY

Parsley may be one of the most useful herbs in the kitchen, but its usefulness doesn't start there. It's a very good companion plant in the vegetable patch too. Allow some of your parsley to flower and it will attract predatory wasps to the garden which will devour harmful aphids. It's often planted alongside asparagus beds as it's thought to see off asparagus beetle, and some believe that when planted among roses it intensifies their scent.

Seasoned spice rubs

Easy to make and a terrific way of adding instant flavour, spice rubs are great, simple gifts for keen cooks. Rub a fine sprinkling of the mixture into the meat about 30 minutes before cooking.

Myrtle spice rub

This blend is particularly good with venison, though it goes well with duck too.
Makes 1 x 50g jar.

2 tablespoons fresh thyme leaves
2 tablespoons fennel seeds
2 tablespoons pink peppercorns
6 myrtle berries or juniper berries
2 cloves
40g sea salt flakes
12 myrtle leaves
½ teaspoon freshly grated nutmeg

1 small jar

With a pestle and mortar, pound together the thyme, fennel seeds, peppercorns, juniper or myrtle berries and cloves, until you have a fairly coarse mixture. In a small bowl, stir in the mixture with the salt, mytle leaves and nutmeg. Tip into a small jar and leave for a week for the flavours to blend. Be sure to remove the myrtle leaves before cooking as they can leave a bitter taste – you're simply infusing the rub with their flavour.

Coriander spice rub

This mixture works extremely well with roasted or barbecued pork.
Makes 1 x 50g jar.

3 tablespoons coriander seeds
3 tablespoons cumin seeds
1 tablespoon black peppercorns
2 teaspoons chilli flakes
40g sea salt flakes
4 tablespoons granulated sugar
3 tablespoons light muscovado sugar

1 small jar

In a dry frying pan, lightly toast the coriander and cumin seeds until just fragrant, about 30 seconds. Then, with a pestle and mortar, pound together the coriander, cumin and peppercorns until you have a fairly coarse mixture. Stir in the chilli flakes, salt and sugars. Tip into a small jar and leave for a week for the flavours to blend.

Both of these rubs keep, sealed in a jar, for up to 3 months.

PACKAGING IDEA
If you like, write the recipe for the spice mixture on the back of the gift tag or card, so when they've used up all of the rub, your friends can make their own.

GROWING MYRTLE Myrtle, *Myrtus communis*, with its glossy, evergreen leaves and pretty white flowers, is an attractive addition to any garden. Plant it in well-drained, fertile soil in a sunny spot. It can be quite tender, so cover it in fleece during the worst of the winter frosts. Alternatively, plant it in a large pot and bring indoors for the winter. Be careful not to over-water myrtle – it hates soggy feet – and prune it lightly in spring to retain an attractive shape. All parts of the plant are fragrant. Used sparingly, the spicy, sweet leaves are an interesting alternative to bay leaves and the flowers can be tossed into salads. You can also substitute the shiny black berries for juniper. Don't discard your prunings, as the wood adds a delicious aroma to the barbecue. The leaves are also very good in pot-pourri (see page 89).

Herbal bathtime 'teas'

These teas aren't a warming infusion which you sip while you bathe – though they do smell good enough to drink; rather they're fragrant little sachets to drop into your bathwater. Each blend makes about 8 sachets.

SLEEPY BLEND

10 tablespoons dried chamomile
5 tablespoons dried lavender

MOROCCAN SPICE BLEND

6 tablespoons dried rose petals and/or buds
3 tablespoons dried lemon verbena
2 tablespoons dried mint
1 thumb of fresh ginger, approx. 7cm long, peeled and grated
6 cardamom pods, roughly crushed
Finely grated zest of 1 small orange
¼ teaspoon ground cinnamon

Muslin
Small, tie-on gift tags (optional)
Needle and thread or sewing machine

Mix all the ingredients together in a bowl, or in two bowls if you are making both versions.

Cut out 16 (or 32) 10cm squares of muslin. Write the name of the blend on the gift tags, if using. Place two squares of muslin together and, either by hand or with a sewing machine, stitch around three sides of the squares about 1cm in from the edge. Spoon a couple of tablespoons of the mixture into the resulting bag. Sew together the final side, making sure you catch the string from the gift tag in the stitching if using. Make the rest of the bags in the same way.

An alternative way to make the sachets is simply to cut the muslin into circles about 14cm in diameter, place the herbal blend in the middle, gather the edges together and tie up securely with string.

Stored in an airtight container, the 'teas' will retain their fragrance for a couple of months.

GROWING CHAMOMILE

Chamomile, *Chamaemelum nobile*, is a deliciously sweet-scented perennial herb renowned for its calming properties. Both the leaves and flowers are strongly aromatic. It thrives in well-drained, light, fertile soil in a sunny spot, though it will tolerate some dappled shade. Sow the seeds in spring, scattering them on the ground and covering them with a thin layer of soil. Water well in dry spells and harvest the flowers in summer when they are fully open. After a couple of years, lift plants in the spring and divide them to promote vigorous growth (see page 10). *C. nobile* is also known as the 'plant physician', as it is said to strengthen the growth of neighbouring plants.

Herb cushion

Certain herbs have long been associated with promoting calm and peaceful sleep. A small pillow filled with hops, lavender and chamomile, either singly or in combination, is a wonderful addition to any bedroom. Herb cushions make great gifts for frequent travellers too, as they are soothing on long flights and provide a welcome touch of home in strange hotel rooms. Makes 1 cushion, approx. 22 x 30cm.

30g dried hops
30g dried lavender
30g dried chamomile

2 pieces muslin, approximately 24 x 32cm
About 0.5m covering fabric
Ribbons or bands of contrasting fabric for trimming
  (optional)
Needle and thread or sewing machine

Combine the hops, lavender and chamomile in a bowl. You may wish to alter the balance of ingredients slightly until you get a combination which you particularly like.

Pin the muslin rectangles together and sew around three and a half sides, either by hand or using a machine, approximately 1.5cm in from the edge. Turn out the cushion liner and stuff with the filling. Sew up the opening.

To make the cover, cut out one piece of fabric measuring 25 x 33cm to form the front of the pillow. If you want to sew on decorative bands of contrasting fabric or ribbon, it's easier to do that now. Cut out two pieces of fabric measuring 25 x 20cm. On the two smaller pieces, turn over the shorter edge by 1.5cm, press and stitch to form a hem.

Place the larger piece on the table, right-side up. Place the shorter pieces on top, overlapping and with the right-sides down, with the hemmed edges towards the middle (when you turn the pillow out, these will form the opening). Pin then stitch, about 1.5cm in from the sides. Trim off the corners, turn out and press. Stuff with the herbal cushion.

GROWING HOPS

Hop, *Humulus lupulus*, is a twining herbaceous perennial which will ramble and climb along wires or across a pergola, providing a striking screen of green. In late summer, female hops bear attractive, papery, lime-green cones which you can dry and use as garlands in the house or to fill pillows. To ensure vigorous growth, plant hops in well-drained, deep, rich soil in a sunny spot, though they will still do pretty well in clay and will tolerate some shade. Plant in winter when the plant is dormant and cut down in autumn to encourage strong growth the following year. *H. lupulus* 'Aureus', the golden hop, is a particularly attractive variety, with deeply lobed yellow leaves.

Fabric conditioner

A bottle of fabric conditioner may seem like an odd gift, but combine it with a Moth-banishing pelargonium (page 113) or Moth-repellent sachets (right) and it makes a thoughtful present for a fashion-conscious friend. Makes 500ml.

Large bunch of basil or mint
Strip of orange, lemon or pink or yellow grapefruit peel, pared with a vegetable peeler and any traces of white pith removed
500ml distilled white vinegar
Pretty bottle

Vinegar not only softens clothes as well as any expensive fabric conditioner, it also helps to remove soap residue which can dull the colours of your clothes. Also, unlike commercial conditioners, it removes stubborn odours rather than simply masking them. And, as an added bonus, if you live in a hard-water area, using vinegar conditioner regularly helps to stop the build-up of limescale in your washing machine.

Crush the basil or mint gently in your hands to help to release its scent, then put the whole stems into a bottle with the strip of citrus zest. Top up with the vinegar.

Pour about 100ml into the conditioner dispenser of the washing machine for each wash.

Moth-repellent sachets

These little sachets are so simple to put together, they're a great creative project for children to make as gifts for clothes-loving godparents or relatives. Makes 8–10.

30g dried wormwood
30g dried lavender flowers
20g dried mint
20g dried rosemary

OTHER THINGS YOU CAN ADD
Dried pelargonium leaves (see page 113 for varieties)
Dried tansy
Dried lemon verbena
Whole cloves
Broken cinnamon sticks

Muslin or light cotton fabric
Tailor's chalk or a soft pencil
Pinking shears (optional)
Ribbon

Combine all of your chosen ingredients in a bowl.

Draw circles of 14cm in diameter onto the fabric using chalk or a soft pencil – use a saucer as a template if you like. Cut out with pinking shears to create an attractive, non-fraying edge, or cut a straight edge with ordinary scissors. Place a couple of spoonfuls of the herb mixture into the centre of each circle and tie into a little bundle with the ribbon.

The sachets will retain their moth-banishing abilities for up to a year, after which time they will need to be replaced.

GROWING BASIL Sweet basil, *Ocimum basilicum*, is a tender annual which needs plenty of sunshine and shelter to thrive. Sow the seed in spring directly into pots and cover with a very fine layer of soil, water and place on a sunny window sill. Put the pots outside in late spring when all chance of frost has passed. Keep pinching out the tips to prevent flowering and promote bushy growth and water in the middle of the day. When the air cools in autumn, bring the pots inside and keep them in a bright corner of the kitchen so you can continue to chop at them into the winter. Some varieties you may like to try are *O. b.* var. *purpurascens*, or opal basil, which has highly fragrant, purple leaves, and *O. b.* var. *minimum*, or Greek basil, which is a compact, attractive little plant with small leaves and excellent flavour.

Antiseptic vinegar

This is a simple version of Four Thieves Vinegar, a concoction which was said to have been used by looters during the plague in 17th-century France to protect them from infections. Use it to clean kitchen surfaces or to soothe grazes or small scolds. Makes 1.5 litres.

A small handful of each of the following fresh herbs/flowers:
Mint
Lavender
Rosemary
Sage
Thyme
Wormwood

1.5 litres cider vinegar or distilled white vinegar
Large jar/bottle with a vinegar-proof lid
Spray bottle or other bottle with vinegar-proof lid
Muslin
Funnel

Roughly chop or tear the herbs, then place in a large jar or bottle and pour the vinegar over to cover. Seal and place in a cool, dark place for 2 months, shaking every now and then.

Line a sieve with muslin and strain the infusion into a large jug. Use a funnel to decant into a spray bottle.

If putting the antiseptic directly on the skin, mix it half-and-half with distilled water. You can make this dilute version ahead of time and keep it in a sterilised dropper bottle for when you need it.

The vinegar will keep for up to a year in a cool, dark place.

Fragrant firelighters

A basket of natural 'firelighters' makes a wonderful hostess or housewarming gift. Make them in autumn when you're pruning back your herb beds and shrubs and you should be able to make enough bundles to last through the winter.

CUTTINGS FROM
Bay
Bergamot
Eucalyptus
Lavender
Lemon grass
Lemon verbena
Mint
Rosemary
Sage
Thyme

OTHER THINGS YOU CAN ADD
Strips of orange, grapefruit, lemon or lime peel
Cinnamon sticks

Raffia or cotton string

Tie the cuttings up in small, mixed bundles with the raffia or string. Leave in a cool, airy place to dry out completely before using them. You could use a drying screen (see box on page 90) or simply hang them upside down from a coathanger until dried, which should take a week or so.

GROWING EUCALYPTUS

Eucalyputus is a genus of more than 400 fast-growing evergreen trees. If you want branches that remain at a low-enough level to cut for flower arrangements and firelighters, you will have to be ruthless about cutting back the previous year's growth to ground level each spring and growing it as a shrub rather than as a tree. It prefers rich soil and full sun, though it is fairly hardy in our climate. If it looks as though it has died during a cold winter, be patient as new stems may well emerge in late spring. One of the easiest varieties to grow is *Eucalyptus gunnii*, or cider gum.

Nourishing herbal face wash

As well as being beautifully fragrant, orange blossom water is a simple and effective skin cleanser. Combined with soothing herbs, it makes a gently foaming face wash which is particularly suitable for dry or mature skins. Look out for pretty bottles, especially those made from dark or opaque glass, to make this face wash and the other beauty products in this book into even more special gifts. Makes approx. 400ml.

5g dried mint or chamomile or thyme
   or borage leaves
2 teaspoons runny honey
100ml orange blossom water
80ml glycerine
80ml liquid pure Castile soap
1 tablespoon witch hazel

Muslin
Funnel
Pretty bottle/s

Place the dried herbs in a small pan with 200ml water. Bring to the boil, lower the heat and simmer gently for a couple of minutes. Remove from the heat, stir in the honey and leave to cool and infuse for an hour.

Line a sieve with muslin and strain the infusion, squeezing the muslin to extract as much of the herbal water as possible. Mix with the rest of the ingredients, then pour through a funnel into the cold, sterilised bottle/s.

The face wash will keep for up to 2 weeks.

GROWING HERBS AND FLOWERS FOR BEAUTY TREATMENTS OR COOKING

It's very important that leaves or petals you intend to use on your skin aren't sprayed with pesticides or other harmful chemicals. Research natural methods of pest control such as vigilant 'housekeeping', companion planting and organic sprays.

38

Herbal vinegar hair rinse

Rinsing once a week with cider vinegar is an excellent way to remove product build-up on hair, leaving it soft and glossy. A hair rinse is a particularly good gift for a friend who lives in a hard-water area, where calcium in the water can make the hair flat and dull. Combined with a bottle of Herbal Face Wash, this makes a very good pampering present. Makes approx. 350ml.

400ml cider vinegar

ONE OF THE FOLLOWING

10g fresh sage leaves (good for weak, dull or dry hair)

10g fresh rosemary leaves (good for dark and/or oily hair)

10g fresh chamomile flowers and leaves (good for fair hair or irritated scalp)

10g fresh marigold petals (good for dull or dry hair)

Muslin
Funnel
Bottles with vinegar-proof lids

Place the vinegar and your chosen herbs or flowers in a small pan and bring to just below boiling point. Leave to cool and infuse overnight. Line a sieve with muslin and strain the vinegar through it. Use a funnel to decant into cold, sterilised bottles and seal with vinegar-proof lids.

To use the hair rinse, massage a teacupful into freshly shampooed hair, leave for a minute and then rinse well.

The hair rinse will keep for up to 4 months.

SAGE AS A COMPANION PLANT

It's a good idea to plant sage alongside carrots and brassicas as it deters carrot fly and cabbage moth. Its flowers also attract bees and other beneficial insects to the garden.

GROWING LAVENDER IN CONTAINERS

Many types of lavender grow well in pots. Container growing is particularly suitable for more tender varieties such as *Lavandula canariensis*, *L. viridis*, *L. pedunculata* or *L. pinnata*, which need to be brought inside during winter in colder climates. Good drainage is very important, so make sure there are broken crocks in the bottom of the pot and mix some extra coarse grit in with the compost. Feed with liquid fertiliser during the flowering season but water sparingly in the winter, allowing the compost to dry out almost completely between waterings.

Sugar body scrub

This body scrub is very simple to make but feels enormously luxurious to use, like something you might find in a smart spa rather than in your kitchen cabinets.

Makes 1 x 250g jar.

150g caster sugar
50g demerara sugar
15g dried rose petals
15g dried lavender flowers
8–10 drops rose essential oil
8–10 drops lavender essential oil
120ml sweet almond or jojoba oil
1 tablespoon glycerine

1 x 250g jar

In a bowl, whisk together the sugars, rose petals and dried lavender. Sprinkle on the essential oils and mix. Trickle over the almond or jojoba oil and glycerine and stir until well mixed. You may want to add slightly more almond oil until you get the texture you want. Scrape into a cold, sterilised jar with a spatula and seal.

The scrub can be used all over your body, but is particularly effective on hands, feet and dry patches such as elbows and knees. Massage in for a minute or two, then rinse off.

The scrub will keep, sealed, for up to a year.

Lavender nail oil

Nourishing lavender oil rubbed regularly into the cuticles helps to keep nails healthy. This makes a thoughtful present for a keen gardener – we all know that, despite our best intentions, many of us forget to wear gloves during long hours toiling in the garden and our hands can suffer as a result. Makes approx. 300ml oil.

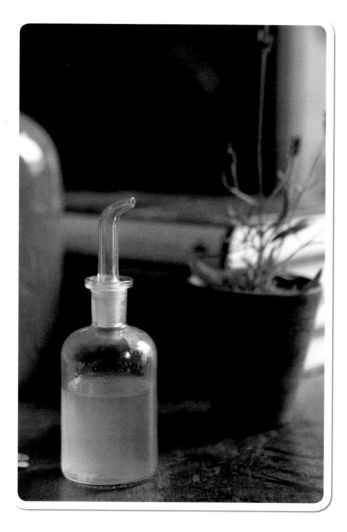

400ml sweet almond oil
50g dried lavender
4 vitamin E capsules

Muslin
Pretty bottles

Pour the almond oil into a pan with the lavender. Warm over a very low heat until small bubbles appear at the edges of the pan. Keep the heat as low as you can, stirring from time to time, and continue to warm for 20 minutes – you don't want to boil the oil, you're simply infusing it with the lavender. Remove from the heat and leave to cool and infuse overnight.

Line a sieve with muslin and place it over a bowl. Strain the oil, pressing down on the lavender to extract as much of the oil as you can. Pierce the vitamin E capsules with a pin and stir the contents into the lavender oil. Pour into cold, sterilised bottles.

The oil will keep for up to 4 months.

REVIVING NEGLECTED LAVENDER PLANTS

Though lavender is fairly simple to grow, without a small amount of regular attention plants can become straggly. In late spring, when the plant begins to put on new growth, cut back the shooting stems by about a third, being careful not to cut into old wood as this won't revive. In early autumn, trim lightly into shape again.

Lavender bath salts

The minerals in sea salt and Epsom salts help to soothe tired muscles and the lavender relaxes a weary mind. This makes a very good gift for anyone going through a trying time. Makes approx. 630g.

300g sea salt
300g Epsom salts (available from some chemists' shops)
2 tablespoons rosehip oil
8 drops lavender essential oil
25g dried lavender flowers

Glass jars

In a large, wide bowl combine the sea salt with the Epsom salts. Sprinkle on the rosehip oil and lavender essential oil and mix with your hands until well combined. Scatter the dried lavender over the top and mix again. Spoon the salts into cold, sterilised jars and seal.

A handful or two of the salts scattered under running water is enough for a relaxing bath.

The salts will keep well for a year.

LAVENDER TROUBLESHOOTING

If your lavender isn't as full and healthy as you would like it to be, it's probably down to two things: soil and location. In the right conditions, it isn't a demanding plant to grow, so give yourself the best chance of success by picking the sunniest spot you can and, if your soil is at all heavy, prepare the ground by digging in some grit or sand to provide it with the fast-draining conditions it loves. Planting lavender near a wall gives it some added warmth and protection from harsh winds in winter.

LAVENDER AS A COMPANION PLANT

Lavender attracts bees and other beneficial pollinating insects to the garden and it is thought to confuse some moths and aphids with its strong scent. It is believed that planting lavender near fruit trees may help to deter codling moth.

PACKAGING IDEA Tie a wooden or aluminium scoop to the jar with a pretty ribbon.

Lavender ironing spray

Anything which makes this humblest of household tasks more enjoyable is surely to be welcomed. This also makes a very good, refreshing room spray. If you have handfuls of lavender in the garden, you can make a simple infusion. For a stronger-smelling spray, add some essential oil and a splash of vodka to help it disperse evenly throughout the liquid; this version also has a longer shelf life, which may be important if you are planning to give it as a gift. Moths hate the smell of lavender, so if you know someone who is suffering from an invasion of these greedy pests, give them a bottle of this spray teamed with some Moth-repellent Sachets (page 35) for a doubly effective present. Makes approx. 750ml.

4 tablespoons dried lavender flowers and leaves
10 drops lavender essential oil
2 tablespoons vodka

Coffee filter paper
Funnel
1 x 750ml bottle, for storing
Spray bottle, for using

Put the lavender into a jug and pour in 250ml of just-off-boiling water. Leave to steep for 5 minutes, then strain through the filter. Add a further 500ml boiled water.

Pour through a funnel into a cold, sterilised bottle. Add the essential oil and vodka and give everything a good shake. Decant into a spray bottle before using for ironing. The simple infusion will keep in the fridge for up to 10 days. The stronger spray will keep for up to a month.

Lavender hand warmer

A cosy woollen hand warmer can make even the coldest day seem a little less daunting and is a great winter gift.

Makes 1 hand warmer.

20 x 40cm medium-to heavy-weight
  wool fabric or tweed
Ceramic pie weights
4 tablespoons dried lavender
Embroidery thread

Needle and thread or sewing machine

Cut out the fabric into two circles or ovals, approximately 15cm in diameter. Pin the fabric together and stitch, about 1cm in from the edge, leaving a gap of about 5cm in the stitching. Snip towards the stitching at intervals to help it lie flat when turned out.

Turn the hand warmer out to the right side and press. Fill fairly loosely with the pie weights – you don't want the hand warmer to be too full, as it needs to sit comfortably in the hands. Spoon in the lavender. Stitch together the opening securely.

Use the embroidery thread to create an attractive blanket-stitch border around the edge of the hand warmer. If blanket stitch seems a little ambitious, a simple line of running stitch about 1cm in from the edge looks very good too.

To warm the hand warmer, place in the microwave at full power for 1½ minutes. Do not leave unattended while warming.

HOW TO DRY LAVENDER

Harvest your lavender on a sunny day after the morning dew has evaporated. Cut the stems just above the leaves when the flower buds have good colour and are just about to open – this is when they smell strongest. Tie them in bundles with elastic bands and hang them upside down in a dark, dry place to help preserve their colour and scent. The buds should take a couple of weeks to dry.

LAYERING LAVENDER

Propagating lavender by layering is a good way of increasing your supply of plants. In early autumn, select a long, vigorous stem and bend it towards the ground. Hold it in place with a hoop of wire pressed firmly into the earth and cover with about 4cm of soil. The following spring, when you see signs of new growth, cut the layered plant from its parent plant and pot up. Plant out the following autumn. (See page 11.)

Lavender wine jelly

This jelly is delicious served with roast lamb or pork. Makes approximately 5 x 225g jars.

1.5kg cooking apples
350ml white wine
3 tablespoons dried lavender, plus
   dried lavender sprigs for finishing
Granulated sugar
Juice of 2 lemons

Preserving pan or large,
   non-reactive pan
Jelly bag, plus extra muslin
Glass jars with lids or cellophane covers
Waxed discs

Roughly chop the apples – you don't need to peel or core them. Place them in a large saucepan with just enough water to cover. Bring to the boil, reduce the heat and then simmer, covered, until the apples are very soft; this should take 45 minutes to an hour. Suspend a jelly bag over a bowl and tip the apples into it. Leave them to drip overnight.

Pour the wine into a pan with the lavender (not the sprigs), bring to a simmer, remove from the heat and strain through muslin. Place a saucer in the freezer to chill.

Pour the lavender-infused wine into the strained juice from the apples and measure. For every 600ml juice, weigh out 450g sugar. Tip the sugar and juice into a preserving or other large pan and warm over a medium heat, stirring from time to time, until the sugar has dissolved. Bring to a rolling boil and boil until the setting point is reached, about 15 minutes. It's reached the setting point when you drop a teaspoonful onto the chilled saucer and it wrinkles when you push it with your finger.

Remove from the heat and skim to remove any scum. Stir in the lemon juice. Pour into warm, sterilised jars and add a lavender sprig to each jar. Cover the top of the jelly with waxed discs and then seal the jars with either cellophane covers or screw-on lids.

Stored in a cool, dark place, the jelly will keep for a year.

THE BEST CULINARY LAVENDER

Used sparingly, lavender adds a fragrant depth of flavour to sweet and savoury dishes. Not all lavenders are equal, however, at least when it comes to cooking. If you're growing lavender for the kitchen, stick to English lavender, *Lavandula angustifolia*. Its sweet, slightly citrusy scent and lower camphor content make it the cook's lavender of choice.

STERLISING JARS & BOTTLES When making any kind of preserve, it's essential that the jars or bottles are scrupulously clean. Either use jars and lids while they're still hot from the dishwasher or, if you don't have a dishwasher, boil them in plenty of water for a minimum of 10 minutes. Cleaned jars can be kept warm in a low oven until you're ready to use them. In some cases, such as when you're making drinks or pickles, you need to use cold jars or bottles – sterilise them first then allow them to cool. Chutneys, pickles and any preserves with a high acidic content need to be sealed with vinegar-proof lids.

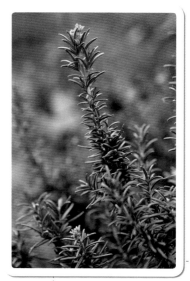

Herb-scented oils

Infusing light oils with herbs and spices is a wonderful way to add instant flavour to salad dressings, roast vegetables and pizzas. Or you can simply pour some into a dish with a little well-flavoured vinegar and use as a dipping oil for bread. Makes approx. 500ml.

500ml light olive oil or sunflower oil
1 teaspoon mixed peppercorns (optional)

FOR ROSEMARY OIL
6–8 sprigs of dried rosemary

FOR THYME OIL
6–8 sprigs of dried thyme or lemon thyme

FOR CHILLI OIL
1 teaspoon chilli flakes
3 whole dried chillies

1 x 500ml bottle or 2 x 250ml bottle/s
Labels

Pour the oil into a heavy-bottomed saucepan and add the peppercorns, if using, and your chosen flavouring. Warm the oil gently over a medium heat just until bubbles appear around the edge of the pan.

Remove from the heat and leave to cool. Pour the oil through a funnel into one or two sterilised bottles. Add the seasonings to the bottle too. Seal, label and leave in a cool, dry place.

The oils will keep in a cool, dry place for 2 months.

SAFETY
Don't be tempted simply to add fresh herbs to oil unless you are planning to refrigerate the oil and use it within 5 days. Using fresh herbs in the oil can lead to the growth of harmful bacteria and is potentially very dangerous.

PACKAGING IDEA Tie some beautiful salad servers to a bottle of flavoured oil, or give a bottle or two with a salad bowl for an extra-special gift.

GRowInG RoSEMARY

It is impossible to imagine a herb garden without rosemary. *Rosmarinus officinalis*, the woody, evergreen hardy perennial, is native to the Mediterranean, so it thrives best in light, well-drained soil where it can bask in sunshine. In spring, after it has flowered, trim it back enthusiastically to ensure bushy growth. In winter, in cooler, less well-sheltered places, it's a good idea to mulch the area around your rosemary to protect it from frost. There is a rosemary for every spot. *R. o.* 'Miss Jessopp's Upright' is a vigorous, bushy variety which makes a splendid hedge; *R. o.* Prostratus Group has a spreading habit, which makes it good for planting in walls, containers or hanging baskets.

Rosemary moisturising lotion

This lightly scented cream can be used on the body but is gentle enough to use on the face too. Makes approx. 250ml.

1 tablespoon fresh rosemary leaves
150ml sweet almond or jojoba oil
1 tablespoon beeswax, grated
1 tablespoon runny honey
2 tablespoons rosehip oil
¼ teaspoon benzoin tincture (a natural preservative)
2 x 125ml dark glass jars

Muslin

Place the rosemary leaves in a small pan with 150ml water. Bring to the boil, reduce the heat and simmer for 5 minutes. Remove from the heat and leave to infuse for 4 hours.

Place a small heatproof bowl over a pan of barely simmering water; the bottom of the bowl should not touch the water. Pour the almond or jojoba oil into the bowl with the beeswax. Warm, stirring from time to time, until the wax has melted. Remove the bowl from the heat, whisk in the honey and cool to room temperature. Stir in the rosehip oil.

Place a sieve over a jug and line with muslin. Strain the rosemary liquid into a jug and stir in the benzoin tincture. Spoon the oil mixture into a food processor or blender and process for a minute. With the motor still running, pour the rosemary infusion through the feed tube and process until you have a smooth emulsion. Transfer the cream into cold, sterilised jars and seal.

This cream will keep in the refrigerator for 2 weeks.

GROWING ROSEMARY FROM CUTTINGS

Rosemary is tricky to grow from seed, but you can increase your supply of this most valuable of herbs by propagating with cuttings. Take softwood cuttings of 10–15cm long from the new wood in spring. Remove the leaves from the bottom of the stem, leaving only about six leaves at the top. Prepare a pot with well-draining compost to which you have added some grit and proceed as for Taking Softwood Cuttings (page 9).

PROPERTIES OF ROSEMARY

Rosemary has strong antiseptic and anti-inflammatory properties. It improves blood flow and refreshes the mind. It is used in beauty preparations to condition the scalp and hair, tone and balance oily skin and reduce puffiness. Its bracing scent uplifts and helps shake off sluggishness, which makes the moisturiser and toner very good for perking up the complexion in the morning.

Rosemary hair oil

This is an intensely nourishing and moisturising hair treatment, perfect for dry, damaged hair. It makes a good gift for anyone who has returned from a summer beach holiday, when the combined effects of sun, salt and chlorine can leave the hair in less-than-pristine condition.

Makes 200ml oil, enough for 5–6 applications.

200ml coconut oil
4 tablespoons rosemary leaves stripped from the stalks
4 drops rosemary essential oil
200ml bottle

Muslin
Funnel

Place the oil in a small pan with the rosemary and bring to a bare simmer over a low heat. Continue to poach the rosemary very gently for 5 minutes, then remove the pan from the heat. Leave to cool and infuse for 24 hours. Line a sieve with muslin and place over a jug. Strain the infusion into the jug and stir in the essential oil. Decant into a cold, sterilised bottle using a funnel.

To use the oil, warm a couple of tablespoonfuls either in the microwave (be careful not to get it too hot) or in a glass placed in a bowl of hot water. Wet the hair thoroughly with warm water and massage in the oil, starting at the scalp and working it through to the ends. Cover the hair with a shower cap and relax for 30 minutes before shampooing the treatment out and rinsing well.

The oil will keep in a cool, dark place for a month.

> ## PACKAGING IDEA
> Pack a bottle of rosemary toner and a jar of rosemary moisturiser into a box or basket with a small rosemary plant. Tie a tag to the plant pot with suggestions for what to do with the sprigs. Aside from the usual culinary uses, a sprig or two tied in a bundle under a running hot tap infuses bathwater with its refreshing, enlivening scent.

Rosemary toner

This refreshing toner is a great way to wake up the skin in the morning and is particularly beneficial to oily skin.

Makes approx. 450ml.

300ml rose water
1 small strip of orange zest, pared with a vegetable peeler, all traces of white pith removed
3 sprigs of mint
2 small sprigs of rosemary
200ml witch hazel
¼ teaspoon benzoin tincture (a natural preservative)
2 x 225ml dark glass bottles

Muslin
Funnel

Place the rose water, orange zest, mint and rosemary in a small pan. Warm over a medium heat and let it cook at a bare simmer for 5 minutes. Remove from the heat and leave to infuse for 4 hours. Line a sieve with muslin and pour the infusion through it into a jug. Whisk in the witch hazel and benzoin tincture. Use a funnel to decant into cold, sterilised bottles.

Use cotton-wool pads soaked with some of the toner to cleanse the skin.

The toner will keep in the refrigerator for 2 weeks.

Scented wax polish

Of course, you can use drops of essential oils to scent your wax polish, but if you have handfuls of herbs in the garden, you can use them to infuse the wax. Strongly scented herbs such as lavender, lemon verbena and rosemary not only smell delicious, but they deter insects too. Makes 1 x 300g jar.

250ml jojoba or apricot kernel oil
15g dried lavender, lemon verbena or rosemary
2 strips of lemon zest, pared with a vegetable peeler,
   all white pith removed
80g beeswax, grated
6 drops lavender or lemon essential oil
Tin or glass jar

Muslin

Place the oil and dried lavender or herbs and zest in a small pan and warm over a very low heat until tiny bubbles just appear around the edge of the pan – do not let it boil. Heat very gently for 5 minutes. Remove from the heat and leave to infuse overnight.

Strain the infused oil through a fine sieve lined with a single layer of muslin into a heatproof bowl which is the right size to fit over one of your pans. Fill the pan with a few centimetres of water – the water shouldn't touch the bottom of the bowl – and bring to a gentle simmer. Place the wax in the bowl with the infused oil and place the bowl over the pan. Warm gently, stirring from time to time, until the wax and oil have melted together and are well blended. Stir in the essential oil.

Pour the polish into a tin or jar. If using a glass jar, warm it in a low oven for a few minutes immediately beforehand to stop it from cracking when the hot wax is poured in.

To use the polish, rub on a small amount – a little goes a very long way – and buff to a sheen with a soft cloth.

The polish keeps for up to a year.

GROWING LEMON VERBENA

Lemon verbena, *Aloysia triphylla*, is a highly useful and versatile herb, worth growing not only because it's very attractive, but also because it's almost impossible to buy commercially. Lemon verbena is a half-hardy deciduous perennial. It comes from Chile, so it likes warmth and should be protected from frost. Prune lightly after flowering and mulch around the base in winter to protect the roots from the cold. It will lose its leaves in winter, so don't be alarmed. Lemon verbena can be propagated from softwood cuttings (see page 9) taken in spring or from semi-hardwood cuttings taken in late summer (see page 54).

Tisane planter

Tisanes (herb infusions) are simple to make and a refreshing alternative to fermented teas. A planter crammed with infusible herbs makes a deliciously enticing gift.

GOOD HERBS FOR TISANES

Chamomile, leaves and flowers
Lavender, leaves and flowers
Lemon balm leaves
Lemon verbena leaves
Peppermint leaves
Rosemary, leaves and flowers
Sage, leaves and flowers
Thyme and lemon thyme, leaves and flowers

OTHER SUITABLE INGREDIENTS

Thin strips of lemon or orange zest,
  any white pith removed
Honey, for sweetening

Infusions of fresh herbs can sometimes have a greater vitality than dried ones and you can choose your herb to match your mood. Peppermint is great after dinner as it aids digestion, lemon verbena, lavender and chamomile are wonderfully soothing, rosemary is enlivening and sage is good for sore throats. You can use the herbs alone or in combination. Add strips of citrus zest if you like, and honey to sweeten.

When planting up your herbs, make sure that the container has suitable drainage holes and place a layer of broken crocks in the bottom. Fill with a peat-free compost mixed with some granular feed in the proportion suggested by the manufacturer. Space the herbs far enough apart to allow them to expand and encourage the recipient of your planter to water it frequently, as container-grown plants dry out more quickly than those grown in the soil. Also, to keep the plants compact and bushy, they should be snipped at regularly. Eventually, most herbs will outgrow a small container so they should either be potted on into larger, individual pots or planted in the ground.

To make a tisane, take a small handful of fresh leaves and blossoms and pour over about 400ml just-off-boiling water. Leave to infuse for 4–5 minutes before straining into a cup. Sweeten with honey if you wish.

TAKING SEMI-HARDWOOD CUTTINGS

Lemon verbena, *Aloysia triphylla*, can be propagated from softwood cuttings (see page 9) taken in spring or from semi-hardwood cuttings taken in late summer through to early autumn. Take a stem of about 15cm, remove the lower leaves and trim off the soft tip and proceed as for softwood cuttings, but using a potting medium which is half seed compost and half sharp sand or perlite. Water well and allow the pot to drain completely, then cover with a plastic bag. Place in a cool place, such as a cold greenhouse or on a shady windowsill. Water sparingly. In spring, when all chance of frost has passed, harden off for a couple of weeks before potting on or planting out.

A trio of tisanes

Making a special tisane (herbal tea) blend is a great way
of showing a friend you're thinking of them.

Energising
The perfect, uplifting
tisane to combat that
late-afternoon slump.

25g dried peppermint leaves

5g dried marigold petals

5g dried ginger

2 pieces of dried lemon grass,
    roughly chopped

2 strips of dried orange zest, pared
    with a sharp vegetable peeler and
    all white pith removed

Dark-coloured glass jars, pots or
    airtight tins

Muslin and string (optional)

Calming
A soothing blend which
helps promote sleep.

20g dried chamomile

10g dried lemon balm

5g dried catmint

5g dried lavender

5g dried rose petals (optional)

Digestive
Serve this blend
after dinner.

20g dried peppermint leaves

10g dried lemon verbena leaves

½ teaspoon fennel seeds

Make up your blend and tip into a dark-coloured jar or an airtight tin to help
preserve the flavour. Alternatively, cut some circles of muslin, spoon a couple
of teaspoons of the blend into the centre of each one and tie into bundles
with string.

All tisanes are better made with water which is just off boiling, so let the
kettle boil, then leave it for a couple of minutes before preparing the infusion,
allowing a generous teaspoon of the blend per person and one for the pot.

The herbal teas will keep, stored in a cool, dark place, for a couple of months.

PACKAGING IDEA
Write out instructions for
making the tisane on a gift
tag. Add a pretty teapot and
tea cup, with perhaps a jar of
honey to sweeten the blend, to
make this into a very special
present indeed. If you were
feeling very generous, add a
tea strainer too.

GROWING LEMON GRASS
Zesty, invigorating lemon grass is essential to many Asian stir-fries and
soups, but it's also very good in tisanes. It can be grown from seed, but it is
a little fiddly and you may need a heated propagator to ensure germination.
Alternatively, and much more simply, take fresh, fat lemon grass stems
you've bought from the greengrocer and place them in a glass of water.
As long as they haven't been over-trimmed, it's a fairly simple thing to get
them to sprout roots. Once the roots are about 4cm long, pot them up and
water thoroughly. Plants will thrive outdoors in full sun. Bring them inside
in the winter, to either a sunny window sill or heated greenhouse, and cut
back on the watering – you want to keep the soil barely moist.

Lemon verbena jelly

This is a subtle and elegant jelly, suitable for a refined friend who may want something a little different for their afternoon tea. It's also delicious brushed on roast chicken towards the end of the cooking or added to pan juices to make gravy. Makes 4 x 220g jars.

45g lemon verbena leaves stripped from the stalks, plus 4 tablespoons of finely shredded leaves
1kg cooking apples
Juice of 2 lemons
Zest of 1 lemon, pared in strips with a sharp vegetable peeler, all traces of white pith removed
Approx. 600g granulated sugar
Glass jars

Preserving pan or large non-reactive saucepan
Jelly bag or muslin

Place 40g of the verbena leaves in a pan with 400ml water and bring to the boil. Boil for 1 minute then leave to cool and infuse. Strain through a sieve into a jug. Discard the leaves.

Don't peel or core the apples; simply chop them into chunks and place them in a large saucepan with the lemon verbena infusion, lemon juice and zest, and just enough water to cover. Bring to the boil and simmer, partially covered, for an hour or so until the apples are very soft and pulpy.

Tip the apples into a jelly bag and suspend over a bowl. If you don't have a jelly bag, place a large circle of muslin in a colander over a bowl, pour in the apples, tie up and suspend over the bowl. Leave to drip for at least 4 hours or overnight. Place a couple of saucers in the freezer.

Finely chop the remaining whole lemon verbena leaves. Measure the juice and return to the clean preserving pan. For every 600ml juice, add 450g sugar. Heat gently, stirring, until the sugar has dissolved. Increase the heat and boil rapidly for 10–15 minutes until the setting point is reached. You can test this by dropping a teaspoon of the jelly onto a chilled saucer and pushing it with your finger – when it wrinkles, it's ready. Remove the pan from the heat, skim off any scum and leave to cool for 10 minutes. Stir in the lemon verbena leaves and pot up in warm, sterilised jars.

Mint jelly

There isn't a finer accompaniment to a leg of roast lamb than this most traditional of English jellies. Including a pot of fresh mint makes this into an even more generous gift.

Makes approx. 5 x 220g jars.

1.5kg cooking apples
5–6 sprigs of mint, tied with kitchen string, plus approx. 40g mint leaves removed from the stalks and finely shredded
250ml cider vinegar or white wine vinegar
Approx. 700g granulated sugar
Glass jars with vinegar-proof lids

Preserving pan or large, non-reactive saucepan
Jelly bag or muslin

Chop the apples into chunks – don't bother to peel or core them. Put them into a preserving pan or large saucepan with the bundle of mint sprigs and just enough water to cover. Bring to the boil and simmer, partially covered, until the apples are soft and pulpy, about 1–1½ hours. Add the vinegar and boil for a further 5 minutes.

Tip the apples into a jelly bag and suspend over a bowl. If you don't have a jelly bag, place a large circle of muslin in a colander over a bowl, pour the apples into it, tie up and suspend over the bowl. Leave to drip for at least 4 hours or overnight. Place a couple of saucers in the freezer.

Measure the juice and return to the clean preserving pan. For every 600ml juice, add 450g sugar. Heat gently, stirring, until the sugar has dissolved. Increase the heat and boil rapidly for about 10–15 minutes until the setting point is reached. You can test this by dropping a teaspoon of the jelly onto a chilled saucer and pushing it with your finger – when it wrinkles, it's ready. Remove from the heat and skim off the scum with a slotted spoon. Stir in the shredded mint and cool for 10–15 minutes (this ensures the shredded mint will be distributed evenly through the jelly, and won't all rise to the top) before potting up in warm, sterilised jars. Put lids on straight away and store in a cool, dark place.

Both of these jellies will keep for up to a year.

Mint soap

If you're making a gift for a sleepy head, this combination of mint and ginger is guaranteed to wake up the senses during a morning shower. Makes approx. 4 soaps.

200g glycerine melt-and-mould soap base, available online from soap-making suppliers
1 tablespoon dried mint
1 tablespoon peeled and grated fresh ginger
5 drops peppermint oil
Sweet almond or groundnut oil, for greasing the moulds

Bain-marie (optional)
Metal or silicone cake tins, or soap moulds

Grate the soap base with the coarse side of a box grater and place in a heatproof bowl. Alternatively, use a bain-marie. Place the bowl over a pan of barely simmering water – the water should not touch the bottom of the bowl. Melt the soap, stirring from time to time, until it's liquid and well blended. Remove the bowl from the heat. Stir in the mint, ginger and peppermint oil and mix thoroughly.

Lightly but thoroughly grease the moulds with a little oil. Pour the liquid soap into a jug and then into the moulds. Rap the moulds gently on the worktop to eliminate air bubbles (though this isn't necessary if you are using silicone moulds) and leave to set for at least 4 hours.

If you're using silicone moulds, simply press the soaps out. If using metal moulds, use a small, sharp knife to help ease them out. Leave in a cool, dry place for 3–4 weeks to 'cure' or harden before using.

GRoWInG MInT

Members of the hardy perennial mint family (*Mentha*) flourish in moderately rich, moist soil in partial shade, though they will tolerate full sun so long as you can guarantee them enough moisture as they are thirsty plants. Mint can be invasive, so if space is an issue, plant your mint in a large pot or bucket with the bottom cut out and sink it into the ground to limit its creeping roots. In spring, divide established plants (page 10) and chop away at it ruthlessly during the summer to encourage new, fresh shoots. Mint will also hybridise promiscuously, so plant different kinds well away from one another.

PACKAGING IDEA Create a pampering mint-themed gift by packing up some of these soaps with a jar of Energising Tisane (page 57) and some Moroccan Spice Blend Bathtime 'Tea' (page 31).

DIFFERENT KINDS OF MINT

There are hundreds of different kinds of mint, though broadly speaking they divide into two groups: peppermint (*Mentha piperita*) and spearmint (*Mentha spicata*). Spearmint, or garden mint, is the one we use most often in the kitchen; it is the mint that we stir into sauces to go with roast lamb or sprinkle over new potatoes or freshly cooked peas. Peppermint is more bracing and pungent. It is very good in teas and cocktails or summery soft drinks. Of the many other varieties, some you may wish to try are:

APPLE MINT (*M. suaveolens*)
Has a distinct aroma of ripe apples. Good in fruity puddings.

CHOCOLATE MINT (*M. x piperata citrata* 'Chocolate') Attractive purple-green leaves and a clean peppermint flavour with a chocolaty accent. Delicious in chocolate puddings.

MOROCCAN MINT (*M. spicata* 'Moroccan') Has a slightly spicy aroma and is a very fine mint to infuse in tea or use in salads.

PINEAPPLE MINT (*M. suaveolens* 'Variegata') An attractive, variegated mint with a sweet, fruity flavour.

Catmint mice

These little mice will delight your feline friends.

Scraps of strong cotton fabric, corduroy or tweed
String or ribbon, for the tails
Hollow fill fibre toy stuffing, available from
  craft suppliers
2 teaspoons dried catmint for each mouse
Scraps of felt for the ears
Embroidery thread, for the eyes

Pins
Needle and thread or sewing machine

For each mouse, cut a heart-shaped paper template, approximately 18cm at its widest point. Pin this to your fabric and cut round it. Cut the fabric heart in half along the central point so that you have two pieces. Place the right sides of the fabric together and tuck the tail in position so that you catch it as you sew around the mouse. Pin together and stitch, leaving a gap of about 3cm in the base of the mouse. Turn the mouse right-side out and press.

Fill the mouse with the hollow fill fibre and a couple of teaspoons of dried catmint, then sew up the hole in the base securely. Cut small triangles of felt for the ears and stitch them on. Embroider small crosses for eyes. The catmint mouse's scent will remain strong for several months.

GROWING CATMINT

Hardy perennial catmint, *Nepeta*, gets its common name from the near-narcotic effect it has on cats, but it makes a very attractive border plant in its own right. Plant in well-drained soil in sun or light shade and when the first flowers have faded, cut right back to within a few centimetres of the soil line to encourage lush growth and a second crop of flowers. If you are cultivating it for your cat, you'll need to protect it. Cats will roll around on the plants in a state of ecstasy and gnaw the foliage down to the stems. Poking some twigs or sticks into the ground around the plant and tying some garden twine in a web between the sticks can help stop the worst of the damage.

Parsley dog biscuits

Giving people presents is one thing, but sometimes puppies need presents too. Parsley is famously good at sweetening the breath, which can only be a good thing.

Makes about 32 bones.

A big bunch of parsley, about 120g, finely minced, stalks and all
1 large carrot, grated
60g Cheddar, or any other strong, hard cheese, grated
3 tablespoons olive oil
300g wholemeal flour
150–200ml hot chicken stock or water

6–8cm biscuit cutter, bone-shaped if possible

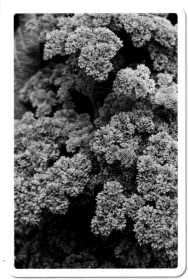

Preheat the oven to 180°C/gas 4 and line a couple of baking sheets with baking parchment.

Stir together the parsley, carrots and cheese. Trickle over the oil and mix. Place the flour in a separate bowl. Tip the parsley mixture into the flour and mix everything up with your hands until well combined.

Gradually add the stock or water, mixing until you have a good, stiff dough – you may not need to use all of the liquid. Knead it together gently with your hands, turn it out onto a lightly floured surface and roll out until it's about 5mm thick. Cut out the dog biscuits, using a biscuit cutter. Knead the offcuts together, roll them and cut them out too. Lay them on the baking sheets.

Bake for about 25 minutes until the biscuits are solid to the touch and turning golden around the edges. Cool on a wire rack.

Stored in an airtight tin, the biscuits will keep for a couple of weeks.

GROWING PARSLEY

Hardy biennial parsley, *Petroselinum*, is possibly the most widely used of all the culinary herbs, so it's worth sowing in successive spring and summer plantings to guarantee a continuous supply. Plant in rich, well-drained soil in a lightly shaded spot. Keep cutting at your plants to ensure vigorous growth, trimming the larger, outer leaves first. *P. crispum* is the curly variety most often used as a garnish and *P. crispum neapolitanum* is an Italian flat-leafed variety with a stronger, more distinct flavour.

PACKAGING IDEA Why not use the biscuit cutter as a useful and unusual gift tag?

GROWING CHAMOMILE FROM SEED

Chamomile Treneague (*Chamaemelum nobile* 'Treneague') and double-flowered chamomile (*C. nobile* 'Flore Pleno') can be propagated only by cuttings or division in spring, but Roman chamomile (*C. nobile*) is easily grown from seed. In early spring, sow the seeds finely in a prepared seed tray and cover with perlite. Provide warmth beneath the trays of 19˚C with a heated propagating mat. Harden off and plant out in late spring when all chance of frost has passed.

Chamomile bubble bath

This mixture can be poured under a running tap to create a gently foaming, moisturising bath. Castile soap is renowned for its mild, non-irritating, cleansing qualities. Traditionally made from olive oil, it's now also sometimes made with other plant-based oils. In its solid or liquid form, it's a very good thing to have in your gift-making kit as it can be used in many beauty and household preparations. Makes approx. 600ml.

4 tablespoons dried chamomile flowers
1 strip of orange zest, thinly pared with a vegetable
    peeler and all white pith removed
1 cinnamon stick
120g pure Castile soap, grated, or 100ml liquid Castile soap
3 tablespoons witch hazel
2 tablespoons glycerine
1 tablespoon powdered gelatine
Pretty bottles

Muslin
Funnel

Put the chamomile into a small pan with the zest, cinnamon stick and 400ml water. Bring to the boil, lower the heat and simmer for 15 minutes. Strain through a sieve lined with muslin.

Add the grated or liquid soap to the infusion and stir until well combined, or until the grated soap has dissolved into the mixture. Stir in the witch hazel and glycerine. Sprinkle the gelatine over the top, leave for a minute and then stir until completely dissolved into the mixture. When completely cold, pour through a funnel into cold, sterilised bottles.

The bubble bath will keep for 4 months.

Chamomile hair rinse

An infusion of chamomile will, with frequent use, help soothe an irritated scalp and bring out the natural highlights in blond hair, making it a suitable gift for fair-haired friends.
Makes approx. 900ml, 3–4 applications.

20g dried chamomile flowers
5g marigold petals (optional)
½ teaspoon benzoin tincture (a natural preservative)
Pretty bottles

Muslin
Funnel

Place the chamomile and marigold petals, if using, in a pan with 1 litre water. Bring to the boil and simmer, partially covered, for 15 minutes. Remove from the heat and leave the mixture to cool and infuse for 4 hours. Place a sieve over a bowl or large jug and line with muslin. Strain the infusion and whisk in the benzoin tincture, then decant into cold, sterilised bottles using a funnel.

After shampooing and conditioning the hair, pour a cupful of the rinse over the hair, starting at the roots and massaging it through to the tips. Leave the rinse in the hair and style as normal.

The hair rinse will keep in the fridge for up to a week.

Pretty tin plant pots

Sometimes, either while away on holiday or shopping in well-stocked delicatessens, we buy tomatoes, puréed chestnuts, oatmeal, olive oil and other foods in such pretty tins it seems a shame to toss them into the recycling after using them. Give them a new lease of life as plant pots for herbs, small flowers and cut-and-come-again salad leaves. They make an original gift for friends who only have a small amount of outdoor space, such as a balcony or window sill.

A selection of tin cans
Small pebbles or broken crocks, for drainage
Potting compost
Herbs, cut-and-come again salad leaves, or
    small flowers such as pansies, pinks and alpines

Hammer and large nail

If you can't find tins with pretty designs printed on the side, plain aluminium cans with the paper labels peeled off can also look surprisingly good.

Wash the tins and dry them. Turn them over and use the hammer and nail to punch a few drainage holes in the bottom. Put a thin layer of pebbles or small crocks in the bottom for drainage, then add compost and pot up your chosen plant.

Many plants will outgrow their tins eventually, but until they do they will make a striking display on a sunny kitchen window sill, either indoors or out.

GROWING TARRAGON

French tarragon (*Artemesia dracunculus*) is, along with chervil, parsley and chives, one of the *fines herbes* of classic French cooking. It's essential to béarnaise sauce, makes a very good seasoning for vinegar and is delicious with egg, fish and chicken dishes. To grow it successfully in a small pot, give it a little shade, don't overwater it and keep pinching out the leaves. When it outgrows its pot, plant it outside in light, well-drained soil in a sunny spot.

Edible wreaths

If you have abundant herbs and chillies in the garden at the end of the summer, preserve them in easy-to-make wreaths. Fresh, they make lovely green (or red) gifts which endure throughout the winter as the herbs and chillies dry and can be snipped off as required. The wire you need is available from good florists' shops.

Generous handfuls of bay leaves, rosemary,
   sage, thyme
Red and/or green chillies

Heavy-gauge wire, available from florists, or an
   old wire coat hanger
Medium-gauge wire, available from florists
Disposable gloves, for handling the chillies
Secateurs

Make a circle using the heavy-gauge wire, winding the ends together to bind. A diameter of about 20cm works well – don't make it so large that you can't cover it generously with herbs and/or chillies.

Lay out the herbs on your work surface in separate piles. Divide each pile into fat little bunches. Cut lengths of the medium-gauge wire of approximately 14cm. Tie each bunch of herbs together with the wire and then attach to the circle, overlapping them so that the stems and wire are covered, until you've completed the circle.

If you want to add chillies to your wreath, start by putting on your gloves, then thread pieces of wire through the top of each chilli. Tie them into the wreath. Alternatively, chillies on their own make very striking wreaths. Simply thread medium-gauge wire through the tops of the chillies until you have a length of about 40cm. Twine the ends together to fix into a circle.

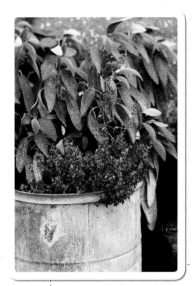

GROWING SAGE

Common sage, *Salvia officinalis*, is native to the Mediterranean and thrives in well-drained soil in a spot where it will enjoy full sun for a good part of the day. Cut back the plant to about half its size after it has finished flowering to keep it vigorous. Though common sage is the version most often used in cooking, there are enormously attractive purple, variegated and tricolour sages which look beautiful in the herb garden. They are milder in flavour than common sage and a little more tender, so may need protecting from harsh frosts in winter.

Sticky sweet cicely buns

Sweet cicely seeds add a hint of anise flavour to these sticky buns. They're a delicious contribution to take along to a brunch or afternoon tea. Makes 12.

1 tablespoon fresh sweet cicely seeds
450g strong white bread flour
1 teaspoon salt
1 teaspoon ground cinnamon
½ teaspoon freshly grated nutmeg
7g sachet fast-action yeast
Finely grated zest of 1 small orange
50g caster sugar
80g butter, melted and cooled
2 free-range eggs, lightly beaten
150ml tepid milk

FOR THE FILLING

60g dried apricots
½ teaspoon ground cinnamon
85g light muscovado sugar
60g pecan nuts

FOR THE TOPPING

120g melted butter, plus extra for
  greasing the trays
120ml runny honey, warmed, or
  maple syrup
50g light muscovado sugar
80g pecan nuts, roughly chopped

2 baking trays, 40 x 27 x 2cm

Reserve 2 teaspoons of the sweet cicely seeds. Place the rest of the sweet cicely seeds on a chopping board and chop them finely with a knife. If they're more dried than green, pound them until fine using a pestle and mortar.

Sift the flour, salt and spices into a large bowl. Whisk in the chopped sweet cicely, yeast, orange zest and the caster sugar. Make a well in the middle, pour in the butter, eggs and milk and mix until you have a soft dough. Turn out onto a lightly floured surface and knead until silky and elastic. Place in a lightly oiled bowl, cover with a plastic bag and leave to rise until doubled in size. This takes 1–2 hours, depending on how warm your kitchen is.

To make the filling, put the apricots in a small bowl and add just enough boiling water to cover. Leave for 15 minutes, drain, pat dry and chop roughly. Meanwhile, put the reserved whole cicely seeds into a food processor with the cinnamon, muscovado sugar and pecans and pulse until quite fine.

Turn the dough out onto a lightly floured surface and knead it lightly for a minute. Divide it in two and roll each piece into a 20 x 30cm rectangle.

Melt the butter for the topping. Brush some over the rectangles of dough and sprinkle half the nut mixture and half the apricots over each. Press the filling into the dough. Roll each rectangle up into a tight cylinder, starting at the widest end. Cut each roll into six pieces.

Brush the baking trays with melted butter. Mix the melted butter, honey/syrup and sugar together and spoon into the bottom of each tray, spreading it out for an even coating. Scatter over the nuts. Put the buns in the trays, leaving about 2.5cm between each one. Cover with tea-towels and leave in a warm place for 40 minutes until slightly risen.

Preheat the oven to 180°C/gas mark 4. Remove the tea towels and bake the buns for 30–35 minutes until they are golden and feel firm. Immediately turn them over and place on a wire rack to cool.

The buns are best cooled, stored in an airtight container and eaten within a day of baking.

GROWING AND USING SWEET CICELY

It's surprising more of us don't grow this pretty, frondy, frothily-flowered herb. Sweet cicely, *Myrrhis odorata*, is a tall hardy perennial which loves rich, well-drained soil and some dappled shade. Cut back the whole plant after flowering to encourage a fresh new growth of leaves.

All parts of the plant are edible. The long tap roots can be grated and eaten raw in a vinaigrette or rémoulade-type dressing, while the leaves have a sweet, aniseedy flavour and are good mixed into fruit salads or soft creamy cheeses and cucumber dishes. They're also a good addition to soups, stews and omelettes. Sweet cicely leaves make things taste sweeter, so they're very good with rhubarb, gooseberries and other tart fruits as it means you can cut down on the sugar used to cook them. The green, unripe seeds taste a little like fennel seeds and impart a mildly spicy, fresh flavour to baking.

Queen of Hungary water

Legend has it that a magical concoction of herbs and flowers was created in the 14th century for Elizabeth, Queen of Hungary. More than just a perfume, it was drunk and massaged into skin as a cure for everything from rheumatism to gout. While I wouldn't recommend drinking this version, it makes a refreshing skin toner which helps heal blemishes. In summer, keep a spray bottle of this scented water in the fridge and use it as a reviving spritz on hot days. Makes approx. 600ml.

GROWING BERGAMOT

Bergamot, *Monarda*, is a clump-forming herbaceous perennial with dramatically pretty whorls of flowers which are really attractive to bees, hence its common name, bee balm. Both leaves and flowers are highly fragrant. Young leaves and flowers are good in salads or pot-pourri, and a tisane of dried or fresh leaves soothes a sore throat. Start seeds off in trays and cover with a fine layer of perlite; providing some heat from beneath will help germination. When they're large enough to handle and all threat of frost has passed, transplant seedlings into pots and harden off before planting out about 50cm apart. Alternatively, cultivate cuttings in summer (page 9, though there is no need to cover the cuttings with plastic) or root divisions in autumn (page 10). Bergamot likes rich, moist, but well-drained soil in sun or partial shade. Cut down the stems in autumn and divide the plant every 3 years or so to remove the dead centre.

A handful of fresh rose petals
A small handful of fresh marigold petals
5 sprigs of rosemary
5 sprigs of bergamot
5 sprigs of peppermint
5 sprigs of lemon balm
5 sprigs of lemon verbena
2 sprigs of sage
A strip of orange zest, pared with a sharp vegetable peeler, all white pith removed
A strip of lemon zest, pared with a sharp vegetable peeler, all white pith removed
Approx. 500ml vodka
Approx. 150ml rose water
Approx. 150ml witch hazel
Pretty bottles

Large glass jar

Layer all of the petals, herbs and zests in a tall, sterilised jar. Pour over enough vodka to cover and leave on a sunny window sill for a couple of weeks, shaking from time to time. Strain and measure the liquid. To each 300ml liquid, add 150ml rose water and 150ml witch hazel. Decant into the cold, sterilised bottles.

The Queen of Hungary water lasts for up to 4 months.

PACKAGING IDEA Pack a generous bottle of Queen of Hungary water into a pretty basket with a perfume spray bottle, so the recipient can decant some of the mixture into it and keep it in the fridge as a sweetly scented enlivener.

Poppy anti-wrinkle wash

For centuries, poppy petals have been prized for their skin-soothing and smoothing properties. Combined with aloe vera, they produce a very good and gentle face wash for more mature skin. Makes approx. 350ml.

A handful of fresh field poppy petals
250ml orange flower water
4 tablespoons pure liquid Castile soap
2 tablespoons aloe vera gel
1 tablespoon glycerine
6 drops grapefruit seed extract (a natural preservative)
4 drops neroli essential oil
Dark glass bottle/s
Muslin

Place the poppy petals in a bowl and pour over enough boiling water to cover. Cover the bowl and leave for 4 hours.

Place a sieve over a jug and line with muslin. Strain the poppy liquid, then gently whisk in the rest of the ingredients. Pour through a funnel into cold, sterilised bottles.

The face wash will keep for up to a week out of the fridge, 2 weeks if refrigerated.

PACKAGING IDEA
Include a small pot of poppy seeds with the face wash. A teaspoon of seeds can be combined with a tablespoon or two of face wash to transform it into a gently exfoliating face scrub.

GROWING POPPIES
Field poppies, *Papaver rhoeas*, love sunshine and well-drained soil. They hate being transplanted. Sow them in spring and autumn directly into the ground, cover them with a fine layer of soil, firm them in very gently and water well. When the seedlings are large enough to handle, thin them out to about 15cm apart. Keep them well watered and deadhead to prevent self seeding. Dry the seeds and use them in baking.

Thyme & fennel seed cleanser

Fennel seeds are very effective at reducing puffiness while thyme has a naturally astringent quality. This mild cleanser would suit any skin type. Decant it into a pretty bottle, which makes an enduring gift after the cleanser has been used up. Makes approx. 300ml.

1 tablespoon fennel seeds
10g fresh thyme sprigs
1 teaspoon runny honey
Juice of ½ lemon, strained
¼ teaspoon benzoin tincture
  (a natural preservative)
300ml dark glass bottle

Pestle and mortar or spice grinder
Muslin or coffee filter paper
Small funnel

In the pestle and mortar or spice grinder, pound or blitz the fennel seeds until fine. Place in a heatproof bowl with the thyme sprigs and pour over 350ml boiling water. Cover and leave to infuse for 30 minutes.

Place a sieve over a jug or bowl and line with muslin or a coffee filter paper. Strain the infusion, pressing down with the back of a spoon to extract as much of the liquid as possible. Whisk in the honey, lemon juice and benzoin tincture and pour through a funnel into a cold, sterilised bottle. Seal and refrigerate.

The cleanser should be applied to the skin on a cotton-wool pad and left for a minute or two before rinsing off with tepid water and patting dry with a soft towel.

This will keep in the refrigerator for a week.

GROWING THYME

There are hundreds of different varieties of thyme. All love well-drained, poor soil and plenty of sun, ideally in a spot where they'll be protected from harsh winter winds. Some of the smaller, creeping thymes, such as *Thymus serpyllum* 'Annie Hall', *T. s.* 'Lemon Curd' and *T. s.* 'Pink Chintz', are very good planted in gravel or in the cracks in paving where they will spread in low mounds and scent the air as you brush past them. Common thyme, *T. vulgaris*, or lemon thyme, *T. citriodorus*, are the most useful in the kitchen. *T. citriodorus* has a sprightly lemon scent and both flowers and leaves are great in cooking, used as a refreshing tisane or added to pot-pourri (page 89). *T. c.* 'Golden King' is an excellent variegated variety. *T.* 'Doone Valley' is lemon-scented and, though it doesn't have such a fine flavour, in spring it is covered in very pretty flowers which, like all thyme flowers, are loved by bees. Propagate by cuttings or division in spring or summer (page 10), or by layering in autumn (page11). After flowering, give the plants a trim to encourage bushy growth and prevent them from becoming woody.

Simple table decorations

While it may be traditional to take a bunch of flowers as a gift for your host, your kindness may leave them with the headache of finding an appropriate vase just when they want to concentrate on pouring drinks and introducing guests. Small plants cultivated in your garden and planted up in pretty pots make a very personal gift. As table decorations for your own dinner party, they benefit from being low in height so they don't distract, and you can even add labels to make them into fragrant place markers which guests can take home with them. Small flowers look good, though if they're going on the dining table it's best to avoid very strongly scented ones. Herbs make very pretty, inexpensive table decorations. You could even reflect the herbs used to season the meal. Use either low-growing herbs, such as thyme or chamomile, or tiny specimens of larger ones, such as bay or lavender.

PACKAGING IDEA

Old, weathered terracotta pots always look pretty, but use your imagination and you can use many easy-to-find containers for planting up your table decorations. Jam jars, pretty tins, old bowls or enamel mugs all look good. Simply fill the bottom with potting compost, pot up your chosen plants and water lightly.

TAKING THYME CUTTINGS

There are over 300 varieties of thyme, and all are neat of habit, fragrant and, when smothered in their tiny flowers, much beloved of bees – indeed, collecting different varieties of thyme can become something of an obsession. They are also easy to propagate from cuttings. In spring or early summer, take a softwood cutting (page 9) of about 8cm and pot up in compost. Bring the cuttings into the house or keep them in a cool greenhouse over winter and plant out the following spring. Alternatively, creeping thymes are easy to divide. They put out aerial roots and form new little 'plantlets' which can be dug up and planted in pots.

SUITABLE FLOWERS
Daisies (*Bellis perennis*)
Dwarf cyclamen
Dwarf irises
Grape hyacinths
Primroses
Snowdrops
Violets

SUITABLE HERBS
Basil
Bay
Chamomile
Chervil
Lavender
Lemon verbena
Thyme
Rosemary

Selection of planters
Potting compost

Pot up your chosen plants and water lightly – if they are in containers with no drainage holes, you don't want to drown them.

The plants will be happy like this for a week or so. After that, they will need to be potted on into containers, which have drainage holes or planted out in the garden.

Caraway flatbreads

These flatbreads taste very good with cheese or served with dips. They're a great gift to take along to an informal drinks party. Makes about 24.

240g strong white bread flour, plus more for dusting
½ teaspoon baking powder
2 teaspoons caraway seeds
½ teaspoon sea salt flakes
A few grinds of black pepper
50ml olive oil, plus extra for oiling the baking sheets

Preheat the oven to 170°C/gas 3 and lightly oil two baking sheets.

Sift the flour and baking powder together, then stir in the caraway seeds, salt and pepper. Trickle the oil over the surface of the flour and rub it in with your fingers. Slowly pour in up to 120ml cold water, mixing as you go – add just enough to make a soft dough. Knead lightly to ensure everything is well combined.

Lightly dust the work surface with flour and roll out the dough until it's about 5mm thick. Use a wine glass or 6cm pastry cutter dipped in flour to cut out circles of dough, then roll out each circle into a long, thin oval.

Place the ovals on the baking sheets and bake for about 5 minutes, until dry and crisp but still fairly pale. Cool completely on a wire rack and then store in an airtight container.

The flatbreads keep well for about 5 days.

GROWING CARAWAY

Caraway, *Carum carvi*, is a hardy biennial which thrives best in rich, well-drained soil in full sun. The seeds are ready for harvesting in the plant's second summer. To harvest the seeds, cut the ripening seed heads off in the morning when the dew is still on them – this will stop the seeds from scattering as you gather them. Cover the seed heads with a paper bag secured with an elastic band and hang them upside down by their stems in a dry, well-ventilated place. The seeds will take about a week to dry out fully.

Drying flowers

Many flowers can be dried quite successfully by hanging them upside down in a warm, dark and well-ventilated place, but using silica gel to dry them will preserve their colours and textures even better. Once dried, they can be used very effectively in wreathes, or wired into posies and table decorations.

SOME GOOD FLOWERS TO TRY

Anemones, asters, cornflowers, daisies, dahlias, delphiniums, freesias, grape hyacinths, marigolds, pansies, peonies, pinks, primroses, ranunculus, roses, snapdragons, zinnias

Silica gel, available from some craft shops and garden centres or online
Large plastic containers with airtight lids
Small, soft paintbrush

Pick the flowers on a dry day after the morning dew has evaporated. Select flowers when they're in as perfect condition as possible for the best results.

Pour a 3cm layer of the gel into the bottom of a plastic container – use separate containers for each type of flower as they may dry at different rates. Place the flowers in the container and gently start to cover them, scattering the gel on gradually and shaking the container to ensure it covers every petal. Once the flowers are completely covered, put the lid on the container, making sure the seal is airtight.

It takes 2–5 days for most flowers to dry. Start to check after a couple of days and, once the flowers are dry, carefully take them out of the gel and remove any remaining granules with a soft brush.

Silica gel can be reused indefinitely. Follow the instructions on the package for reactivating it.

GROWING ANEMONES

The De Caen group of *Anemone coronaria* comes in a wide range of bright colours, from white to deepest purple, scarlet and shocking pink. Their colours remain fairly true when dried in silica.
Plant in winter through to spring to ensure a succession of flowers. Soak the tubers in warm water overnight before planting in light, sandy soil to a depth of twice the height of the tuber and 10cm apart. Mulch in autumn to protect the plants from frost.

GROWING PRIMROSES

Hardy herbaceous perennial primroses, *Primula vulgaris*, brighten up the early spring landscape with their pretty, lightly scented flowers. They will bloom cheerfully in many conditions but do best in well-drained soil in dappled shade. Trim off any dead leaves or blooms to prolong flowering and water well during spring and summer, less frequently from autumn onwards. Primroses grow very happily in pots and window boxes too.

Crystallised flowers

These make pretty and unusual gifts for keen bakers. Make sure you use flowers which have not been sprayed with pesticides or any other chemicals.

SOME LEAVES & FLOWERS SUITABLE FOR CRYSTALLISING

Borage flowers
Dianthus flowers
Lavender flowers
Mint leaves
Primroses
Rose petals
Scented pelargonium leaves and flowers
Violas
Violets

1 egg white
Caster sugar

Tweezers
Pastry brush or small, soft paintbrush
Sugar sifter or tea strainer

In a small bowl, lightly whisk the egg white together with 1 teaspoon cold water. Hold the flower, petal or leaf you want to coat with tweezers and paint completely with the egg white, making sure the whole surface is covered.

Hold the flower, petal or leaf over a baking sheet or some baking parchment to stop the sugar going all over the work surface, then sprinkle the flower with sugar, using either a sugar sifter or tea strainer to scatter it evenly; make sure that the whole surface is covered. Shake off any excess. Place on baking sheets lined with baking parchment and leave in a warm, dry place for several hours or overnight to dry out completely.

Store in an airtight container, placing baking parchment between the layers of flowers, petals or leaves to protect them. They will keep well for several months this way.

Decorated candles

Bought candles decorated with dried flowers and leaves make wonderful gifts which you can tailor to their recipients. Herbs and leaves look very good in minimalist rooms, while a host of petals and flowers suit a more feminine or vintage interior. Delicate, fine foliage works better than fleshier examples.

Paraffin candle wax

Essential oils (optional)

Plain pillar or dinner candles (pale colours generally work best)

Delicate dried flowers and leaves (see Decorated Stationery, page 17)

Double boiler pan (the top part of the boiler should be deep enough for you to dip in the full length of the candle)

Sugar thermometer

Tongs

Small paintbrush

Very soft, lint-free cloth

Paraffin wax is highly flammable, so choose a day when you can give the project your full attention. Select the dried flowers and leaves you want to use to decorate the candles and lay everything out before you start.

Put the wax in the top of your double boiler and put some water in the bottom. Place the sugar thermometer in the pan. Heat gently, stirring with a long metal spoon from time, until the wax is completely melted. Paraffin wax has a melting point of 56–58°C/132–136°F. You can add a few drops of essential oils to scent your candles at this point if you like. Don't leave the melting wax unattended at any point, and when it's melted, remove from the heat.

When the wax has melted, dip the paintbrush into the wax and paint it around the parts of the candle you want to decorate. Gently press the flowers or leaves onto the candle, then brush a little wax over the top to fix it in place. Alternatively, carefully dip the leaves or flowers into the wax and place them on the candle, smoothing gently to fix.

Hold the candle by the wick (you may want to use tongs to do this) and quickly dip the entire candle into the wax to set the decorations. Cool completely and then buff gently to a sheen with a soft cloth.

Note: Never leave burning candles unattended.

Posies and buttonholes

Natural posies of garden flowers are so much more enchanting than the mean and contrived bunches in many of the less imaginative florists' shops. Spoiling your friends with the best your garden has to offer is really one of the most generous gifts of all.

CUTTING FLOWERS

The best time to cut flowers and branches is in the morning, while the dew is still on them. Cut them just before they are in full bloom and they will last longer in the vase. Immediately put them in a bucket of water in a cool, shady place for a few hours before arranging them.

To condition most flowers for arranging, use sharp secateurs to cut the stems again, about 5cm from the base and on the diagonal so they will take up as much water as possible. Remove any leaves which will sit below the water line in the vase to limit the growth of bacteria which will shorten the life of your arrangement.

MAKING A SIMPLE POSY

Strip the foliage from the lower parts of the stems. Hold three or four stems in your hand, arranging them at an angle so they begin to form a spiral. Layer in more stems, again at an angle, turning the bunch frequently to ensure it's a good shape. Hold in place with a rubber band, then tie tightly with raffia or ribbon. Trim the stems so that they're slightly longer in the centre than at the edges.

BUTTONHOLES

Don't save buttonholes just for weddings. And don't truss them up with the ungainly wire and tape used to torture commercial buttonholes into obedience either. Choose flowers and foliage which won't wilt easily, and if you have to fix them with florist's tape, conceal it beneath raffia, thin silk or satin ribbon wound around the stems. Keep it simple. A few hydrangea blossoms, a cornflower, a single stem of lily of the valley will all look fresh and pretty. Or use herbs such as rosemary, a tiny fern frond or some oak leaves and acorns.

GROWING PINKS

Pinks, *Dianthus*, are among the most beloved of the old-fashioned cottage garden plants, largely because of their deliciously sweet and slightly clove-like scent which makes them a particularly good addition to pot-pourri. Plant in a sunny, well-drained spot and water in dry spells. Pinks become woody and sprawling after a while, so renew from cuttings in late spring. Gently tug away non-flowering shoots and trim just below a leaf joint. Put the cuttings round the edge of a pot filled with a mixture of one part potting compost to one part horticultural grit and place in a shady part of the garden, uncovered. Don't overwater or the cuttings will rot. Once they are established, pinch out the tips to create bushy plants which can be planted in the soil in early autumn.

Pot-pourri

Pot-pourri has had a bit of a bad rap in the past few years. Many commercial versions, smothered with artificial fragrances and dyed lurid colours, have all of the appeal of a plug-in air freshener. Making your own from the herbs and flowers in your garden is a different matter altogether. Delicately scented and subtly beautiful, it makes a wonderful present. For wet pot-pourri, look out for old-fashioned pot-pourri dishes with pierced covers to allow the scent to escape. For dry pot-pourri, any attractive dish will do. For advice on highly-scented roses, see page 90.

Wet pot-pourri

Wet pot-pourri mixtures take longer to make, though they are more intensely scented. When the perfume starts to fade, reactivate it by sprinkling on a few drops of brandy and stirring.

Handfuls of rose petals, gathered as the flowers
  come into full bloom
Coarse sea salt
20g each of ground cinnamon, ground allspice and
  ground nutmeg
5g ground cloves
100g powdered orris root, a fixative available online
  or from natural remedies stores
Juice and the finely pared zest of 3 lemons
50ml brandy
20 drops each of bergamot, lavender and
  Rose Maroc essential oils
Large glass jar

During the course of the summer, layer rose petals and salt in a large glass jar – a handful of rose petals to a handful of salt. After a couple of months, mix together the spices, orris root, lemon juice and zest and essential oils with the salted rose petals and any of the other dried flowers and herbs from the list (right). Sprinkle on the brandy. If the mixture seems too wet, sprinkle on some more orris root and mix. Return to the glass jar and store in a cool, dark place for a couple of months to mature before using.

Dry pot-pourri

This is the simpler mixture to make, though its scent fades more quickly than that of wet pot-pourri. It can be revived by sprinkling on more essential oils as needed.

30g powdered orris root, a fixative available
  online or from natural remedies stores
15g gum benzoin powder, a fixative available
  online or from natural remedies stores
1 teaspoon ground cinnamon
30 drops each of bergamot, lavender and
  Rose Maroc essential oils
250g dried rose petals
150g dried lavender flowers
Any dried flowers, herbs and leaves from the list below
Large glass jar

Place the orris root, gum bezoin and cinnamon in a small bowl and sprinkle over the essential oils. Rub them together with your fingers until well blended.

Combine the rose petals and lavender flowers in a bowl with any dried flowers, herbs and leaves from the list below, then scatter over the essential oil mixture and stir until well combined. Store in a large glass jar in a cool, dark place for at least a month before using.

> ### OTHER DRIED FLOWERS & HERBS TO INCLUDE
> (for either the wet or dry pot-pourri): bergamot flowers and leaves, strips of citrus zest, honeysuckle, jasmine, lemon balm, lemon verbena, lavender flowers, myrtle, pinks, scented geranium leaves, sweet Williams, violets and wormwood.

Lip balm

These little pots of lip balm serve a dual purpose, as they work very well as nail and cuticle cream, too. They're good gifts for well-groomed friends, particularly if you package them in shatter-proof containers – they're perfect to carry around in a handbag or brief case. Makes approx. 8 pots.

130ml sweet almond oil
20g dried rose petals, dried mint or dried lavender
70g beeswax, grated
1 teaspoon runny honey
2 vitamin E capsules

Small glass, metal or plastic pots or jars (25ml is a good size). If they're going to be left on a dressing table or in a bathroom cabinet, the sort of miniature jam jars that grace many a hotel breakfast are the perfect size

Place the oil in a small pan with the dried rose petals, mint or lavender. Warm very gently over a low heat for 5 minutes – do not let it boil. Cover and leave to cool and infuse for several hours or overnight. Strain into a small, heatproof bowl and discard the solids.

Place the bowl with the oil in it over a pan of barely simmering water – the water should not touch the bottom of the bowl. Stir in the beeswax and honey until everything is completely melted and blended. Remove from the heat, pierce the vitamin E capsules with a pin and squeeze the contents into the lip balm mixture. Pour into the pots, cool and seal.

The lip balm will keep for 2 months.

Rose & oatmeal facial scrub

This is a very nourishing and beautifully scented facial scrub. Oatmeal removes impurities from the skin and is so gentle that it can be used on the most sensitive of complexions. Makes approx. 60g.

40g rolled oats
20g dried rose petals
4 drops essential Rose Maroc oil
Pretty jar

Place the oats and rose petals in a food processor or blender and pulse several times until the mixture is quite fine. Sprinkle on the essential oil and pulse once more to blend. Spoon into a cold, sterilised jar.

To use the scrub, combine a couple of tablespoons of the mixture with enough water to make a smooth paste. For very dry or sensitive skin, use milk in place of the water. Smooth onto the face and neck, leave for a minute and then massage the scrub into the skin in gentle, circular motions. Rinse off with tepid water and pat dry with a soft towel.

The facial scrub will keep for 4 months.

DETERRING PESTS FROM ROSES

Planting any member of the onion family close to roses deters aphids as they become confused by their strong scent. They may lessen the chance of the leaves developing black spot too. Clumps of chives (page 23), allowed to flower, certainly look pretty among the roses and some believe that neighbouring alliums intensify the perfume of roses too.

PACKAGING IDEA Write a label explaining how to use the facial scrub and tie it around the jar. If your intended recipient really loves roses, combine it with the Rose Milk Bath (page 94).

Rose water

Distilling your own rose water using things you probably already have in your kitchen is enormously satisfying and easy. The rose water on its own makes an original and generous gift, or whisk in a few more ingredients to create a gentle and nourishing cleanser. Makes approx. 850ml.

FOR THE ROSE WATER
Enough heavily scented rose petals to fill a 1-litre jug about three times (see page 90 for good scented varieties)

FOR THE CLEANSER
300ml rose water
1 tablespoon glycerine
1 tablespoon witch hazel
6 drops Rose Maroc essential oil

House brick
Large pan with a slightly domed lid
Heatproof bowl of at least 1-litre capacity
Bag of ice cubes
Funnel
Dark glass bottles

Place the brick in the middle of the pan and put the bowl on top of it. Scatter the petals all around the brick. Pour in just enough water to cover the petals and brick.

Cover the pan with the upside-down lid – inverting it lets the steam drip down into the bowl. Bring the water to the boil and immediately place a few handfuls of ice cubes on top of the pan lid. Lower the temperature and simmer the rose petals and water. The steam will rise, hit the inverted dome of the iced lid, condense and drip down into the bowl.

Every 15 minutes or so, lift the lid and remove a teaspoonful of the rosewater in the bowl to test its strength. When it's ready, it should smell and taste very strongly of roses. Don't let it simmer too long though as its strength will start to decline after 40–50 minutes.

Carefully remove the bowl from the pan and place in a bowl of iced water to chill it as quickly as possible. Use a funnel to decant it into cold, sterilised, dark glass bottles and refrigerate.

To make the rose water cleanser, gently whisk together all of the ingredients and use a funnel to decant into cold, sterilised, dark glass bottles.

Both the rose water and rose water cleanser will keep in the fridge for up to a month.

ALTERNATIVE: JASMINE WATER
If you have an abundance of jasmine blossoms, you can use them in the same way to make a deliciously scented jasmine water. Decant this into a spray bottle and spritz it lightly on your face when you need a pick-me-up, lightly spray it on pillows before sleep or use it as an uplifting room spray. See page 109 for advice on growing jasmine.

THE PROPERTIES OF ROSES
Many of us are familiar with the uplifting feeling of walking through a rose garden on a summer's day, breathing in the sweet and heady scent of the flowers. Rose essential oil has been used in beauty treatments for centuries, since not only does its aroma enhance wellbeing, but, applied to the skin in creams, lotions and oils, it also reduces redness and is very beneficial to dry or sensitive complexions. While rose essential oils are expensive because of the enormous number of flowers it takes to make them, rose water (see left) is a mild and thrifty way of benefiting from the near-magical properties of roses. Though obviously not as intense as essential oil, it has excellent antiseptic, calming and moisturising qualities.

Rose Milk Bath

It's rather satisfying to think that two such humble ingredients as powdered milk and Epsom salts can contribute to such a luxurious, spa-worthy present. Dried milk moisturises the skin while Epsom salts relax tired joints and, it is believed, draw out toxins from the body. Makes 340g.

200g powdered milk
120g Epsom salts, available from chemists
12 drops essential Rose Maroc oil
20g dried rose petals
Pretty, airtight bottles/jars

In a bowl, mix together the powdered milk and the Epsom salts. Sprinkle over the rose oil and mix to combine. Scatter over the rose petals and mix again, then seal in an airtight container. A handful of the milk bath should simply be scattered into running bathwater for a luxurious, relaxing bath. The milk bath will last for up to a year.

Rose hand cream

This sweetly scented, but hard-working cream makes a very good present to give to an enthusiastic gardener. Makes approx. 320g.

100ml sweet almond or jojoba oil
50g shea butter
20g beeswax, grated
100ml rose water
½ teaspoon benzoin tincture (a natural preservative)
4 drops Rose Maroc essential oil
4 drops lavender oil (optional, though it will help heal small cuts
    and scratches on hard-working hands)
Dark glass jar/s

Place a small heatproof bowl over a pan of barely simmering water; the bottom of the bowl should not touch the water. Put the almond or jojoba oil into the bowl with the butter and beeswax. Warm, stirring occasionally, until the wax has melted. Leave to cool to room temperature.

Whisk together the rose water, benzoin tincture and essential oil/s in a jug. When the oil/wax mixture is cool, spoon it into a food processor or blender and process for a minute. With the motor still running, pour the rose water through the feed tube and process until you have a smooth emulsion. Use a spatula to transfer the cream into cold, sterilised jars and seal. This cream will keep in the refrigerator for 3–4 weeks.

Rose petal pistachio meringues

The combination of pistachios and roses gives a rather Middle Eastern twist to this most English of puddings. This recipe is a very good way of using the Rose Petal Sugar on page 98. If you're giving the meringues to a keen cook, tuck a jar of the infused sugar in the box too, so the recipient can make their own. Makes approx. 8 medium-sized meringues.

4 egg whites, at room temperature
240g rose petal sugar (page 98)
1 teaspoon rose water
60g shelled, unsalted pistachios, roughly chopped

Before making your meringues, make sure the bowl and whisk or beaters are scrupulously clean. Line a baking sheet with non-stick baking parchment and preheat the oven to 150˚C/gas mark 2.

Beat the egg whites until stiff. Add the rose petal sugar one spoonful at a time, beating well after each addition, until all of the sugar is used up and the mixture is stiff and glossy. Trickle the rose water and scatter two thirds of the pistachios over the top and quickly and lightly fold in with a metal spoon.

Spoon the mixture onto the prepared baking sheet in generous dollops. Scatter the remaining pistachios over the meringues. Place in the oven and immediately turn the oven down to 110˚C/gas mark ¼. Bake the meringues for 1¼ hours, until you can lift them up from the baking parchment without them sticking. Turn off the oven and leave the meringues in the oven to dry out as the temperature cools.

The meringues will keep in an airtight container for 3–4 days.

PACKAGING IDEA If you're baking these in summer when the roses in your garden are abundant, make up a posy of your best blooms to go with the box of meringues. It makes for a particularly charming gift as home-grown roses are so much more enchanting than bought specimens.

HOW TO PLANT BARE-ROOTED ROSES

If you can, always buy bare-rooted roses. They are more economical and you often have a much wider choice of varieties. They're available by mail order and should be planted as soon as you get them. Soak them in a bucket of water for an hour before planting. Dig a hole about the width and depth of your spade. Fork in some fertiliser, such as chicken pellets, according to the package instructions. Place the rose in the middle of the hole, spreading out the roots. Lie a bamboo cane across the top of the hole and make sure the base of the stems is 2.5cm below soil level. Back-fill with the soil you've dug out of the hole and gently heel the rose in with your foot. Water and mulch around the base of the rose. Prune the stems back to an outward-facing bud about 15cm from the ground.

Rosehip jelly

This deliciously tangy and unusual jelly is very good on toast or scones, combined with some cream cheese or clotted cream. Or stir into the pan juices of roast pork, venison or duck to make a quick gravy. Makes approx. 6 x 220g jars.

600g rosehips, picked over to remove any leaves
1.5g cooking apples
Approx. 900g granulated sugar
Juice of 1 lemon
Jars

Preserving pan or other large, non-reactive pan
Jelly bags or muslin
Kitchen string

Put the rosehips in a food processor and pulse a few times to break them up. Put them into the pan with 300ml water. Gently bring to the boil, partially cover and simmer until the hips are very soft, about 45 minutes to an hour. Place in a jelly bag and leave to drip over a large bowl overnight. If you don't have a jelly bag, place a colander over a bowl, line it with muslin, spoon the rosehips into it, tie up with kitchen string and suspend over the bowl. Don't be tempted to squeeze the bag or the jelly will be cloudy.

Roughly chop the cooking apples without peeling or coring them and place them in the pan with just enough water to cover. Cook gently until they form a soft and fluffy purée, about 45 minutes to an hour. Strain as for the rosehip juice. If you don't have enough muslin or jelly bags to do this simultaneously, you can do it over the course of 2 days, refrigerating the rosehip juice until the apple juice is ready.

Put two saucers in the freezer to chill. Combine the rosehip and apple juices and measure. For every 600ml liquid, weigh out 450g sugar. Put the fruit juices, sugar and lemon juice into the preserving pan and warm over a low heat, stirring until the sugar has dissolved. Raise the heat and boil hard until the setting point is reached. You can check this by dropping a teaspoonful of the jam onto a chilled saucer and leaving for a minute. If it wrinkles when you push it with your finger, it's ready. Remove from the heat, skim off any scum with a slotted spoon, pour into warm, sterilised jars and seal. The jelly will keep in a cool, dark place for up to 2 months.

Scented sugars

Sugar absorbs the sweet scents of petals, leaves and herbs beautifully and can be used to impart a subtle aroma to baking, fruity puddings, ice creams, jams, teas and custards. A selection of scented sugars is a pretty and useful gift for a keen baker. Makes 250g.

FOR EACH BATCH
250g caster sugar

PLUS ONE OF THE FOLLOWING INGREDIENTS
2 tablespoons lavender flowers
A small handful of rose petals
12-16 lemon verbena leaves
12-16 mint leaves
6-8 scented pelargonium leaves
Jars

Pestle and mortar (optional)

Combine the sugar with your chosen seasoning. Bash them together gently in a pestle and mortar or pulse them a couple of times in a food processor to help release the scent. Tip into a jar and seal. Leave for at least a couple of weeks for the flavours to develop and sift before using.

BEST ROSES FOR ROSEHIPS

On country walks, gather the hips from wild dog roses, *Rosa canina*. Alternatively, plant your own *R. canina*, or one of its hybrids, or one of the old *R. rugosa* varieties, all of which have beautiful rosehips in the autumn.

Marigold cheese

Infusing milk with marigold petals creates a simple curd cheese with a beautiful golden colour. It's very good crumbled into salads or spooned onto crackers. You must ensure that the milk you use to make it is either raw (available from some farmers' markets) or unhomogenised, which means a thick layer of cream will rise to the top of the bottle. Makes approx. 400g.

2 litres whole organic milk, raw or unhomogenised
20g dried marigold petals
Pinch of salt
2 teaspoons rennet, available from chemists,
    healthfood shops and some supermarkets

Thermometer (optional)
Muslin

GROWING MARIGOLDS

Marigolds, *Calendula officinalis*, are a great addition to any sunny border and are as easy to grow as they are cheering to look at. They do very well in containers, hence their common name, pot marigolds. In spring, sow the seeds directly into the ground about 25cm apart – ideally in rich, well-drained soil, though they seem to grow fairly contentedly almost anywhere. Deadhead regularly during the summer to encourage more flowers, but be sure to leave some towards the end of the season so that they can self-seed and supply you with an abundance of pretty petals the following year. The petals have a wide range of culinary and medicinal uses and the young leaves can also be added to salads.

Pour the milk into a stainless-steel saucepan and add the marigold petals and salt. Heat the milk gently to 38°C/100°F, or blood temperature. If you don't have a thermometer, you can test this by putting your finger into the milk – it should feel neither hot nor cold. Remove the pan from the heat, stir in the rennet and leave for about 15 minutes. The milk will separate, with the curds rising to the top and the whey remaining at the bottom of the pan.

Line a large sieve or colander with a double layer of muslin. Using a slotted spoon, gently skim off the curds and place them in the muslin. Then tie up the corners and hang the cheese to drip above a bowl or the sink for about 3 hours. If you prefer, you can leave it for up to 24 hours, which will result in a harder cheese. Unwrap the cheese, place it in a bowl, cover and store in the fridge.

Refrigerated, the cheese will keep for about 3 days.

PACKAGING IDEA This simple cheese is the perfect thing to take along to an informal summer lunch or dinner. To transport it, wrap it in a clean circle of muslin and pack it into a small basket. A little posy of freshly picked marigolds makes a charming accompaniment too – they can be used to decorate the table or the fresh petals can be scattered in a pretty salad with the crumbled cheese.

Marigold, honey and oatmeal soap

Soap making can be just as satisfying and addictive as creating delicious recipes. Combine ingredients to suit your mood, whether you want something to uplift, energise or promote relaxation. This is a pretty and soothing concoction. Marigolds are a natural anti-inflammatory, honey nourishes and moisturises the skin and oatmeal is a gentle exfoliant. Cheering, soothing, citrus-based essential oils provide the perfect seasoning. Makes 10 x 50g soaps.

500g melt-and-mould white soap
3 tablespoons runny honey
5 tablespoons dried marigold petals
4 tablespoons coarse oatmeal
10 drops bergamot, neroli or mandarin essential oil
1 tablespoon sweet almond or groundnut oil
Soap moulds, bun tins or small tart tins

Grate the soap with the coarse side of a box grater and place it in a heatproof bowl large enough to fit over one of your pans. Alternatively, you can use a bain-marie. Add the honey to the soap. Place the bowl over a pan of barely simmering water – the water should not touch the bottom of the bowl – and melt the soap with the honey, stirring from time to time, until it's liquid and well blended.

Remove the bowl from the heat. Stir in the marigold petals, oatmeal and essential oils and mix thoroughly. Lightly but thoroughly grease the moulds with a little of the sweet almond or groundnut oil. Pour the liquid soap into a jug and then pour it into the moulds. Rap the moulds gently on the work surface to eliminate air bubbles (this isn't necessary if you are using silicone moulds) and leave to set for at least 4 hours.

If you're using silicone moulds, simply press the soaps out. If using metal moulds, use a small, sharp knife to help ease them out. Leave in a cool, dry place for 3–4 weeks to 'cure' or harden.

PACKAGING New or vintage bun and tart tins in interesting shapes make great soap moulds. You can simply unmould the soaps and pack them in a pretty box or give them in the tins, as an extra little gift for the lucky recipient.

DRYING MARIGOLD PETALS

Pick the marigolds (*Calendula officinalis*) when the flowers are fully open, on a sunny morning after the dew has evaporated. Place them on a drying screen (page 90) in a dry, shady, well-ventilated place and turn them regularly until they are papery. Pull the petals from the buds and store them in a dark glass jar or other opaque container until ready to use. As well as using them to add colour to simple cheeses (page 100), you can infuse them in tea (page 57), scatter them over risottos or pilaffs, or use them in beauty preparations such as the Marigold Face Tonic (page 105).

Marigold face tonic

Marigold petals have natural antiseptic properties and have been used in preparations to promote clear complexions for centuries. This mild toner is suitable for all skin types. Makes approx. 750ml.

25g dried marigold petals
Approx. 350ml witch hazel
4 tablespoons rose water
2 tablespoons glycerine
1 teaspoon benzoin tincture
   (natural preservative)
Pretty bottles

Muslin
Funnel

Place the marigold petals in a glass or ceramic bowl and pour over 500ml boiling water. Cover and leave the mixture to infuse for 3–4 hours. Strain the infusion through a sieve lined with muslin into a jug. Measure and stir in an equal amount of witch hazel, followed by the rose water, glycerine and benzoin tincture. Use a funnel to decant into cold, sterilised bottles.

The tonic will keep for up to a month, or 2 months if stored in the fridge.

TYPES OF MARIGOLDS

The kind of marigolds used in cooking and beauty preparations are *Calendula officinalis*, or pot marigolds, which are renowned for their antiseptic and soothing properties. Don't confuse them with *Tagetes*, more commonly called French or African marigolds. *Tagetes* petals are inedible, but consider planting some anyway as they're among the most useful of all the companion plants. Their roots give off a powerful aroma which deters harmful nematodes and slugs and, planted near tomatoes, they are believed to discourage whitefly.

Sage water skin tonic

Sage is an excellent antiseptic and is very effective at combating oily skin, making this a particularly good gift for a teenager prone to blemishes. Makes approx. 300ml.

20g fresh sage leaves
2 tablespoons cider vinegar
1 teaspoon glycerine
¼ teaspoon benzoin tincture
   (a natural preservative)
Dark glass 300ml bottle

Muslin or coffee filter paper
Small funnel

Bring the kettle to the boil and place the sage leaves in a heatproof bowl, crushing them lightly with your hands to help release their scent. Pour over 300ml boiling water, cover and leave to steep for 20 minutes.

Place a sieve over a jug or bowl and line with muslin or a coffee filter paper. Strain the sage infusion, pressing down with the back of a spoon to extract as much of the sage liquid as possible. Whisk in the vinegar and glycerine and pour through a funnel into a cold, sterilised bottle. Seal and refrigerate.

The tonic should be applied to the skin on a cotton wool pad twice a day after cleansing.

This tonic will keep in the fridge for a week.

Teacup planters

Single teacups can be picked up fairly inexpensively at markets, charity shops and car boot sales. They make perfect, pretty planters for small flowers, foliage and bulbs. You could also use sugar bowls or small milk jugs or teapots. Because of their scale, teacup planters look particularly good on bedside tables, on desks or by the bathtub, where their patterns, colours, textures and scents can be peacefully enjoyed.

SOME SUGGESTIONS FOR TEACUP PLANTERS

Crocuses
Daisies (*Bellis perennis*)
Dwarf cyclamen
Dwarf irises
Lily of the valley
Miniature daffodils, such as
  'Tête à Tête'
Primroses
Small-leaved ivies
Small sempervivums
Snowdrops
Violets

Cup and saucer, or other
  small container
Small gravel, for drainage
Potting compost

Masking tape
Tea towel
Protective goggles
Power drill and small
  ceramic tile bit

To transform your teacup into a planter, you are first going to need to add some drainage. To do this, place a small strip of masking tape in the middle of the interior base of the cup. Turn the cup upside down on a board covered in a tea towel. The board will protect the work surface from the drill bit and the tea towel will stop the cup from moving around. Place some masking tape on the middle of the cup's upturned base and mark the centre of the base with an 'X'. Put on your goggles and, using the ceramic tile bit, slowly drill a hole in the bottom of the teacup. Remove the tape.

Place a thin layer of gravel in the bottom of the teacup and scatter on some compost. Pot up your chosen plant, firm it in gently and water. Once the plant has finished flowering, either discard or plant outside where it may come back the following year.

GROWING GRAPE HYACINTHS

In the middle of winter, the delicate scent and intensely blue flower spikes of grape hyacinths, *Muscari*, are positively heart-warming. Little pots or planters of them dotted around the house promise that spring is imminent.

GROWING BULBS IN TEACUPS

In autumn, scatter some potting compost in your planter (for grape hyacinths, choose a teacup about 8cm deep), then set the bulbs side by side on top, allowing one to three bulbs per cup depending on its size – their tips should be level with the rim of the cup. Scatter some more compost over the top and water sparingly. Next, you need to place the bulbs in a cold (about 4°C/40°F), dark shed or cellar for several weeks, ensuring that the compost is kept barely moist, until shoots appear. This can take 8–10 weeks. Once the shoots appear, bring into the house and water. If you keep the planter in a coolish part of the house and away from strong direct sunlight, the flowers should last 3–4 weeks.

Bath fizzies

You can customise these bath fizzies with dried herbs, flowers and essential oils according to your mood or the person you're giving them to. Chamomile creates a relaxing bath, whereas jasmine is sensual and uplifting. Bath bomb moulds are available from some craft shops and online, but you can also use large silicone ice-cube trays or bun tins. Makes 6-8, depending on the size of the mould.

300g bicarbonate of soda
150g citric acid, available from chemists and online
5 tablespoons dried chamomile or dried
  jasmine flowers
12 drops chamomile or jasmine essential oil
Witch hazel

Spray bottle
Bath bomb moulds or large silicone ice-cube trays
  or bun tins

Sift together the bicarbonate of soda and citric acid several times until everything is well blended. Mix in the dried flowers and sprinkle over the essential oil.

Spray on some witch hazel, stirring the mixture with your other hand as you spray. You need to spray just enough witch hazel to get your fizzies to stick together, but not so much that they start to react and fizz. As soon as the mixture holds together like damp sand when you squeeze it in your hands, place it in your moulds, packing it in quite tightly to ensure a sturdy bath fizzy.

Leave the mixture to set in the moulds for an hour, then turn out onto baking parchment and leave to harden for a few hours or overnight.

The bath fizzies will keep for several months in an airtight container.

GROWING JASMINE

Considering its delicate appearance and heady, exotic scent, jasmine is surprisingly undemanding to grow. Winter-flowering jasmine, *Jasminum nudiflorum*, produces starry, yellow blossoms on its naked stems when little else is in flower, but for scent you really want its summer cousin, *J. officinale*. This deciduous climber needs a warm, sunny site to flourish and will clamber over trellises and pergolas, though it will need the support of wires to grow up against a house wall. Water freely in spring and summer, and prune after flowering to maintain its shape.

PACKAGING IDEA
Wrap the bath fizzies in clear cellophane and tie them with ribbon. Pack several in a basket with other bathtime treats such as the Fennel & Honey Face Mask (page 162) or Cornflower Eye Compresses (page 118).

Almond and lemon-scented geranium biscuits

Using scented sugar gives these simple almond biscuits a more complex and intriguing flavour. If your sweet-toothed recipient is a plant lover too, a pretty pot containing a scented pelargonium (geranium) along with the batch of biscuits makes a great gift. Makes approx. 20.

100g unsalted butter, softened
60g lemon-scented pelargonium sugar (page 98), sifted
120g self-raising flour, sifted
30g ground almonds
2 small lemon-scented pelargonium leaves, finely shredded
Grated zest of ½ small lemon
1–2 tablespoons milk
Approx. 20 whole, blanched almonds

Preheat the oven to 180°C/gas mark 4. Line two baking sheets with baking parchment.

Cream together the butter and sugar until light and fluffy. Beat in the flour, ground almonds, pelargonium leaves, lemon zest and just enough milk to make a firm dough. Shape into walnut-sized balls and arrange on the baking sheets, leaving about 3cm space between each biscuit as they spread out while they're cooking. Slightly flatten the balls and press a whole almond into the top of each one.

Bake the biscuits for about 10–12 minutes until lightly golden around the edges. Allow to cool on the sheets for a couple of minutes before placing on a wire rack to cool completely.

The biscuits will keep in an airtight tin for 3–4 days.

PELARGONIUM VARIETIES

Use this recipe as a starting point and vary the flavour of the biscuits by infusing the sugar with different scented pelargoniums. Some good ones are:

CITRUSY
P. 'Mabel Grey', P. 'Prince of Orange', P. 'Lemon Fancy'

ROSE-SCENTED
P. graveolens, P. 'Attar of Roses'

SPICY
P. 'Fragrans' (nutmeg)

MINTY
P. tomentosum

PACKAGING IDEA If you're giving the biscuits to a keen baker, tuck a jar of the scented sugar into the package, too.

Moth-banishing pelargoniums

There are few more annoying wardrobe problems than unfolding a favourite sweater and finding it has been nibbled by moths. Worse, they really seem to love the good stuff, tucking into cashmere, silk and linen while leaving cheaper, synthetic clothes untouched. If you have a fashionable friend, a moth-banishing scented pelargonium makes a natural, enduring and practical gift. Add a card with instructions on drying the leaves and perhaps some Moth-repellent Sachets (page 35) to get them started.

1 scented pelargonium (see list)
Pretty pot

To dry the leaves, either lay them on a drying screen (make one of these by stretching and stapling fine mesh to an old picture frame) or line a small tray with kitchen paper and scatter the leaves on top to dry. When the leaves are completely dry and quite crisp, store them in a dark, airtight container until you're ready to use them.

The dried leaves can be sewn or tucked into sachets (page 31) and placed in wardrobes or drawers, where their strong smell will deter moths from planting their damaging little eggs. They hunt out fabric by scent, so baffling them with pelargoniums is highly effective.

The best part of giving a friend a living plant is that when the dried leaves lose their potency, they can simply pluck a few more. This benefits the pelargonium too, as it promotes stronger, thicker growth. It really is a houseplant which earns its keep.

BEST MOTH-BANISHING VARIETIES

The following pelargonium varieties make wonderful houseplants, releasing their scent and freshening the air as you brush past them, but their strong scents are less popular with hungry pests. They are believed to deter mosquitoes too, which makes an even more compelling reason to give one a home.

CITRUSSY
'Prince of Orange', 'Orange Fizz', 'Bitter Lemon', 'Queen of the Lemons'

ROSE-SCENTED
'Lady Plymouth', 'Vandersea', 'Attar of Roses', 'Rober's Lemon Rose'

CEDAR-SCENTED
'Painted Lady', 'Clorinda', 'Copthorne', 'Souvenir de Prue'

GROWING PELARGONIUMS

Pelargoniums make very good houseplants, but if you can give them a little holiday outdoors for a few weeks in the summer, it will improve their vigour. Indoors, place the plant in a bright spot where it will receive some direct sunlight for part of the day. In spring and summer, water generously enough that water comes through the drainage holes of the pot but allow the surface of the compost to dry out between watering. Feed once every couple of weeks with a dilute high-potash plant food, such as tomato fertiliser, and take the chance to pick over the plant, removing any dead leaves and fading blooms. In autumn, cut the plant back by half to encourage bushy growth and reduce watering, keeping the soil almost dry through the winter until the plant starts to show signs of new growth the following spring.

Scented room spray

Capture the scents of your garden at high summer in a bottle. Makes approx. 350ml.

20g fresh rose petals
15g fresh scented pelargonium leaves
10g fresh lemon verbena leaves
5g fresh lemon thyme leaves
5g fresh lavender leaves and flowers
100ml orange blossom water or rose water
4 drops each orange, rose and lavender essential oil
1 teaspoon benzoin tincture (a natural preservative)
Pretty spray bottles

Muslin
Funnel

Combine the petals, leaves and flowers with 500ml water and simmer for 15 minutes. Leave to steep, covered, overnight.

Line a sieve with muslin and strain the infused water. Then, in a bowl, whisk together with the orange blossom or rose water, essential oils and benzoin tincture. Use a funnel to decant into cold, sterilised spray bottles.

The spray will keep for about 2 months, up to 4 months if refrigerated.

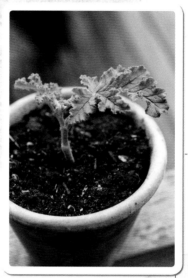

PRoPaGaTIng PeLARGonIUMs FRoM cUTTIngs

There are so many varieties of scented pelargoniums that collecting them can become quite addictive. It's fortunate, then, that they're so simple to propagate from cuttings, which makes them very easy to swap and share with friends. In late summer, take a cutting about 10cm long, cutting just below a leaf joint, and strip the leaves from the lower part with a sharp knife, leaving only two or three leaves at the top of the stem. Fill a 7.5cm pot with a mixture of equal parts seed compost and either fine composted bark or horticultural grit. Make four to six holes 2.5cm deep around the edge of the pot and insert the cuttings. Gently firm them in and water lightly. Place the pot in a warm place out of direct sunlight until they root. Water sparingly while the cuttings take and pot them on once new leaves start to grow.

Pansies in cheese boxes

When I buy soft cheeses, they often come in such pretty wooden boxes I'm reluctant to throw them away. I put them to use as unusual temporary planters for small flowers, such as pansies. They make simple, inexpensive table decorations which I then give away to guests. The small, wooden trugs which smart French butter is sometimes packed in also make very good containers for small plants. If you follow the Victorian language of flowers, pansies are a particularly appropriate gift to give to your friends as they mean 'loving thoughts'. The word pansy derives from the French word pensée, or thought, because their dainty flowers look so much like human faces.

gRowIng PansIes

Pansies, *Viola* x *wittrockiana*, those most cheerful of cottage garden plants, are always a happy sight in the garden, tilting their sweet faces towards the sun. They can be tricky to germinate (though will enthusiastically self-seed once in the garden), but nurseries usually carry such a wide range at relatively low cost, it hardly seems worth the trouble. Enjoy them through the spring, deadheading to encourage more flowers and cutting back when they start to set seed. You may get a second flush of flowers in the autumn.

A selection of wooden cheese boxes or
   butter trugs (different ones look better
   if giving to several guests)
Clingfilm
Potting compost
Pansies, or other small flowering plants
Moss (optional)

Line the cheese boxes with clingfilm and partially fill them with compost. Remove the pansies from their pots and gently transplant them into the boxes. Water very lightly. If you like, you can cover the soil surrounding the pansies with moss.

Obviously, the plants won't thrive in these conditions for long, but you and your guests can enjoy them for a few days before planting them out in the garden.

Cornflower eye compresses

For centuries, infusions of cornflowers have been used to soothe tired and irritated eyes. These cornflower compresses would be a thoughtful gift for a friend who spends long hours at a computer screen, or whose eyes are sore from hayfever or a long flight.

Makes 10, enough for 5 treatments.

Approx. 40g dried cornflower petals (see page 90 for instructions on drying petals)

Muslin
Sewing machine or needle and thread

Cut out the muslin into 20 circles approximately 8cm in diameter. Pin two circles together and stitch about 1cm in from the edge, leaving a gap of about 2cm in the stitching. Spoon a teaspoon of the dried petals into the circle and stitch it closed. Repeat with the rest of the circles.

To use the compresses, place two of them in a small bowl and pour over just enough boiling water to cover. Leave to steep in the liquid until cold. Lie back, place a circle on each eye and relax for 10 minutes. Discard the circles after using.

PACKAGING IDEA Tie the circles together in a bundle with ribbon and place in a pretty box, along with the instructions on how to use the compresses on a label or card. Perhaps add a packet of cornflower seeds too – they're so easy to grow and so striking in the flower bed, it would be difficult to think of anyone who wouldn't love them.

GROWING CORNFLOWERS

Cornflowers, *Centaurea cyanus*, like to grow in well-drained soil in full sun. Sow straight into the ground, in either the autumn or spring, or both if you want to guarantee a long succession of flowers from late spring through the summer. Prepare the soil by raking it over and removing any weeds or stones. Scatter the seeds sparingly and rake them in before giving the area a good water. When the seedlings appear, thin them to about 30cm apart. Keep cutting at the flowers to encourage more blooms. Cornflowers make excellent cut flowers and will last in a vase in the house for a week or more.

centaurea cyanus

centaurea cyanus

CORNFLOWER

Field

Pine-cone garland

If you have a friend whose festive taste leans more towards the natural than the tinsel, this garland is a beautiful gift which will last for many years. Collect pine cones from the garden or on winter walks, and supplement your bounty with cones bought in from garden centres, craft shops or florists' suppliers online.

Paper-covered wire, available from garden centres and florists' suppliers
A large quantity of small pine cones, at least 100
Jute garden string
Dried orange slices (see page 123), optional
Dried apple slices (see page 123), optional
Bay leaves, optional

Large needle, if you're adding orange slices and bay leaves

Cut the wire into 12cm lengths and wrap a length tightly around the base of each cone, concealing the wire in the microsporophylls (that's 'leaves', to you and me) of the cone. Begin tying the cones into the garden string. Tie them in tightly, bunching them up together, so the string is well covered. Trim off the excess wire. If you're interspersing the cones with orange and apple slices and bay leaves, thread the string on the large needle and poke it through the slices and bay leaves. Small bundles of each look better than single specimens.

When you have the length you want, tie a loop at each end of the string to attach the garland to a fireplace, doorframe or stair banister.

Pine-cone firelighters

A bag of these makes a fantastic seasonal gift for any friend who has an open fire. They look beautiful coated simply with the beeswax, but you can colour them red and green by grating a couple of wax crayons in with the wax, if you like. The essential oils are optional but add a lovely seasonal scent. Makes 12.

12 small pine cones
12 paper muffin cases
Waxed wicks or garden string
About 700g wax, either beeswax or paraffin wax
Wax crayons, grated (optional)
Essential oils, e.g. orange, cedar, sandalwood, clove, nutmeg, pine (alone or in combination – optional)

Double boiler, or a heatproof bowl you can fit over one of your pans
Small muffin tray

If you've gathered your own pine cones and they feel a little damp, place them on a baking sheet and dry them out in the oven at 180°C/gas mark 4 for 10–15 minutes.

Line the muffin tray with the paper cases. Tie a length of wick or string around the base of each cone, leaving a tail of about 8cm.

Gently melt the wax (and the grated crayons, if you want coloured wax) in a double boiler or in a heatproof bowl over a pan of simmering water. Don't leave unattended at any point while melting.

When the wax has melted, stir in any essential oils if you're using them. Hang the cones upside down by the wicks and dip them in the wax, making sure you dip some of the wick to. Place them in the centre of the muffin cases, draping the wicks over the sides. Carefully pour or ladle the wax into the muffin cases around the cones, letting it come about half-way up each case. Leave to cool and set.

Tuck a pine cone firelighter in among the kindling before lighting the fire.

Frosted holly leaves

'Frosting' the edge of holly leaves is an easy project which small children might like to help you with. Use the leaves to adorn wreaths (page 123), decorate Christmas wrapping (page 14), or as part of a Christmas flower arrangement. You may well have Epsom salts left over from some of the other projects in this book – they look more natural and subtle than glitter.

Holly sprigs
Glue pen or clear craft glue
Epsom salts

Fill a bowl with Epsom salts. Working with one holly sprig at a time, paint a thin layer of glue around the edges of the leaves. Hold the sprig over the bowl and use a teaspoon to dredge the leaves with the Epsom salts. Place on a wire rack to dry. Continue with the rest of the sprigs.

Christmas wreath

Making your own wreath is guaranteed to get you into the Christmas spirit. It's very simple to do and the results are impressive. I like to use highly scented things to decorate my wreath, such as lemons, cloves and cinnamon, which give a delicious waft of Christmas as you enter the house. Makes 1.

FOR THE WREATH

1 flat-wire wreath, approx. diameter 30–40cm, available from florists, suppliers online or some garden centres
Moss, available from garden centres or florists
Florist's wire, thick and fine gauges
A selection of thin ribbon for tying bundles and wide ribbon for hanging the wreath

TO DECORATE

A selection of: apples, berries, cinnamon sticks, cloves, fir branches (which can be off-cuts from your Christmas tree), eucalyptus, ivy, lemons and/or limes, oranges, pine cones, star anise

Secateurs
Needle and thread
Glue gun, or some strong glue
Staple gun or tacks

First, make the dried orange or apple slices, if you are planning to use them. Slice the fruit very thinly and dry on wire racks in the oven on its lowest setting for several hours or overnight.

To assemble the wreath, begin by covering the wire form generously with moss, then tie it securely using thick florist's wire. Next, tie in sprigs of fir and/or eucalyptus so that the wreath is densely covered. Then wind ivy around the wreath, securing it at intervals with fine florist's wire.

You can use the dried apple and orange slices singly or glued together in stacks of three. Cut a length of fine florist's wire approximately 20cm long and push it through the centre of the apple or orange slice/s, then push it back through about 1cm from the original hole – this will give you a loop of wire to tie the slice/s to the wreath. Cover the wire on the front of the slice/s by gluing on a star anise.

Glue together bundles of cinnamon sticks and wind around a length of fine wire to attach them to the wreath. Cover the wire with ribbon and tie it into a bow. Stud the lemons or limes with cloves and push a length of thick wire through the centre of each, long enough to tie it to the wreath.

Tie lengths of fine wire to the pine cones, berry sprigs and anything else you want to include. Lay it flat on a table and arrange the various elements around it until you have an arrangement you like, leaving space for the ribbon you're going to use to attach it to the door. Tie in your decorations securely, hiding any pieces of wire beneath the fir and ivy. Attach a loop of ribbon at the centre-top of the wreath and sew it on securely, leaving enough of a 'tail' to attach it to the door. Hide the stitches with a generous bow. Use staples or tacks to attach the length of ribbon to the top of the door.

GROWING IVY

Ivy, *Hedera*, is a garden workhorse. It grows in tough places where more refined plants struggle and comes in many varieties, from dainty to bold, rich green, to variegated and golden. In winter it provides a welcome splash of lush colour and sometimes berries, invaluable to birds and insects. Ivies can be grown up walls, trained over tree stumps or in pots or hanging baskets. Generally, the *Hedera* genus prefers a limy soil, so add a handful of lime to the planting hole. Yellow varieties do best in a sunny spot; green or silver varieties do well in shade or sun.

FRUIT, VEGETABLES & NUTS

Crème de cassis

This luscious liqueur is traditionally served with white wine as a kir or with champagne as a kir royale, but it's also delicious poured over very good vanilla ice cream to create a near-instant pudding. Crème de cassis, made in the summer and allowed to mature for a few months, makes a very good Christmas present. Makes approx. 1.6 litres.

700g blackcurrants, picked
    over to remove any stalks
700ml red wine
Approx. 800g caster sugar
Approx. 400ml vodka
Pretty bottles

Muslin
Funnel

Place the blackcurrants in a ceramic or glass bowl and mash lightly with a potato masher. Stir in the red wine, cover with clingfilm and leave to macerate for at least 24 and up to 48 hours.

Purée the blackcurrants and wine in a food processor or blender and then strain through a muslin-lined sieve into a jug. Press down on the fruit with a wooden spoon to extract as much juice as possible. Measure the volume of liquid (you should have about 1 litre), then pour it into a large saucepan. For every 250ml liquid, add 200g caster sugar.

Heat gently, stirring frequently, until the sugar has dissolved. Do not let the liquid simmer, as you don't want to boil off the alcohol. Leave the mixture barely steaming at the lowest heat for an hour or so, stirring occasionally, until the liquid has reduced and become slightly syrupy – you should have about 1.2 litres. Leave to cool.

Mix together 1 part vodka to 3 parts of the cooled blackcurrant liquid. Use a funnel to decant into cold, sterilised bottles. Store in a cool, dark place for at least a month before drinking.

The crème de cassis should be drunk within 2 years.

GROWING BLACKCURRANTS

Blackcurrants, *Ribes nigrum*, are generous croppers – a happy, established bush can provide up to 4.5kg of fruit each year. Plant in fertile, acidic, well-drained soil in as sunny a spot as you can muster, though they will tolerate some shade. Ideally, plant your blackcurrant bush in late autumn or winter and, a couple of weeks before planting, dig some well-rotted manure into the soil. Dig a hole twice as big as the root ball, tease out the roots if you're planting a container-grown specimen, back-fill and firm the bush in well. Mulch with a layer of bark or well-rotted manure to help prevent moisture loss. In the first spring after planting, chop down the stems to two buds above ground level to encourage the growth of new stems.

FRUIT, VEGETABLES

Redcurrant & rose syrup

This makes a delightful gift to take along to a summer party. It's delicious diluted with champagne or over ice with soda water, and if any remains the next morning, your hosts can trickle it over pancakes at breakfast. Makes 3 x 750ml bottles.

A handful of rose petals (see page 90 for highly scented varieties)
350ml fruity rosé wine
1.5kg redcurrants
Approx. 800g Rose Petal Sugar (page 98), sifted
Bottles

Preserving pan or large, non-reactive saucepan
Jelly bag or muslin
Kitchen string
Funnel

Place the rose petals in a pan with the rosé wine. Bring to a simmer, remove from the heat and leave to infuse for 2 hours. Strain into a jug.

Put the redcurrants into a preserving pan with the infused wine and crush them a bit with a potato masher. Bring to a simmer, cover and cook for 30 minutes until the currants are very soft. Remove from the heat and crush again. Spoon the mixture into a jelly bag over a bowl. Alternatively line a colander with muslin, place over a bowl and spoon the currants into the centre; tie up with kitchen string and suspend over the bowl. Leave to drip overnight.

Measure the juice. For every 600ml juice, weigh out 400g rose petal sugar. Put the juice and sugar back into the preserving pan and warm over a medium heat, stirring to dissolve the sugar. When the sugar has dissolved, boil hard for 5 minutes or until sufficiently syrupy. Remove from the heat and skim off any scum with a slotted spoon. Decant into warm, sterilised bottles and seal.

The syrup will keep in the fridge for up to a month.

GROWING REDCURRANTS

Redcurrants, or *Ribes rubrum*, are self-fertile, so you only need one bush to produce a crop. They do best in good, well-drained soil in a sheltered position where they'll receive plenty of sun, but they are remarkably tolerant of less-than-ideal conditions. Mulch in spring with a layer of well-rotted manure, compost or straw. Water regularly in the growing season, until you've finished harvesting the fruit, and keep the ground around the bush as weed-free as possible.

Redcurrants bear their fruit on old wood. Prune in late winter just before the buds begin to swell. Cut back any very old branches to ground level, then prune back new growth to two buds in early summer to keep the bush compact. When the beautiful, jewel-like strings of fruit are ripe, cut whole trusses and use them as quickly as possible as they do not keep well. You may need to throw a net over your bush to stop the birds and squirrels getting to the fruit before you do.

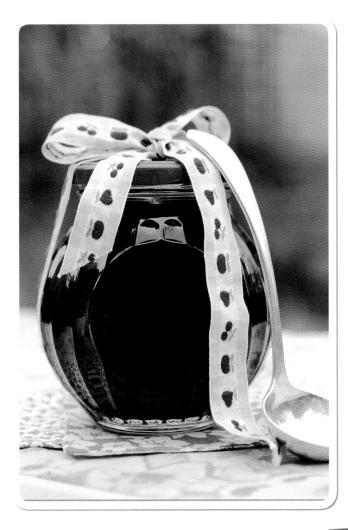

Cherries in brandy

Though a rather luxurious treat to receive, this is a very simple gift to make. A few jars prepared in summer when cherries are plentiful and sweet make great Christmas presents. The cherries can be spooned over ice cream or panna cotta, and the brandy is also very good served chilled in shot or liqueur glasses. Makes approx. 1.2 litres.

500g sweet or morello cherries
Approx. 150g caster or vanilla sugar
500ml brandy

OPTIONAL FLAVOURINGS
A strip of orange zest, pared with a vegetable peeler and all traces of white pith removed or 1 vanilla pod, split
1.2-litre jar

Rinse the cherries and remove the stems, but leave the stones in as this makes for a better flavour and texture.

Place the cherries in a large, cold, sterilised jar, then tip over the sugar. If you are using morello cherries, add a tablespoon or two more of sugar to sweeten. Tuck the orange zest or vanilla pod in among the fruit, if you wish to add more flavour. Pour over the brandy. Seal the jar and shake a few times to help the sugar begin to dissolve.

Store in a cool, dark place for 2 months, shaking the jar from time to time to help the sugar dissolve.

Unopened, the cherries will keep for 6 months. After opening, store in the fridge and eat within a month.

GROWING MORELLO CHERRIES
If you have room for only one cherry tree, make it a morello. Sour cherries, *Prunus cerasus*, of which morellos are a variety, are difficult to buy in the shops and are so delicious in baking, in jams or preserved in brandy. They are also self-fertile and, unlike sweet cherries, *Prunus avium*, which need full sun to develop their optimum sweetness, morellos do well in shady spots and grow successfully against north- or east-facing walls. As an added bonus, they're also less attractive to birds than their sweeter cousins.

Blackberry jam

Whether it's made with gathered or cultivated blackberries, this lovely jam is one of the best flavours of high summer.
Makes about 4 x 220g jars.

500g cooking apples, peeled, cored and diced
500g blackberries
Juice of ½ lemon
700g granulated sugar
Jars

Preserving pan or large, non-reactive saucepan

Place two saucers in the freezer.

Put the diced apples in the preserving pan with 100ml water. Simmer gently for 10 minutes until the apples have broken up into a soft, fluffy pulp. Add the blackberries and lemon juice and continue to cook for about 5 minutes until the blackberries soften and begin to release their juices.

Add the sugar and stir over a low heat until it has dissolved. Bring to the boil and boil rapidly for about 15 minutes, until the jam reaches its setting point. You can test this by spooning a little of the jam onto one of the chilled saucers and leaving it for a moment to cool. Push it with your finger, and if it wrinkles, the jam is ready. Remove from the heat and skim off any scum with a slotted spoon. Spoon into hot, sterilised jars and seal.

The jam will keep, sealed, for up to a year.

For tips on growing blackberries, see page 135.

Fruit cheeses

Fruit cheeses make a great gift for lovers of strong, hard cheeses as they go together beautifully. Use up a glut of orchard fruits or a generous haul of fruit from a blackberry walk. Makes approx. 900g.

FRUITS TO CHOOSE FROM

1.5kg plums (firm ones with some
   tartness rather than ripe dessert plums)
   or damsons, stones removed
1kg blackberries with
   500g cooking apples, diced
750g pears, diced, with
   750g cooking apples, diced,
500g quinces, diced, with
   1kg cooking apples, diced
Granulated sugar
Straight-sided jars or small dishes

Preserving pan or large, non-reactive saucepan
Nylon sieve
Glycerine
Food-grade paraffin wax, for sealing

Put the fruit into the pan with 200ml water. Simmer gently over a low heat until you have a soft, thick pulp. Rub through a nylon sieve, pressing with a wooden spoon to retrieve as much pulp as possible. Weigh the pulp. For every 600g pulp, weigh out 450g sugar.

Put the pulp and sugar into a clean pan and warm over a low heat, stirring, until the sugar has dissolved. Bring to the boil, lower the heat and simmer, stirring frequently, until the mixture is very thick and glossy, about 50–60 minutes.

Brush the inside of the hot, sterilised jars with a little glycerine (this will make it easier to unmould the cheese later) and pour in the fruit cheese. Seal and store in a cool, dark place for at least a month before using. If your containers don't have lids or it's difficult to seal them using wax paper discs and cellophane covers, seal them with melted food-grade paraffin wax. Fruit cheese will keep, unopened, for a year.

GROWING PLUMS

Give plums a fertile, well-drained site in full sun and plant your tree in late autumn/ early winter to give it a chance to establish itself before the weather warms up in spring. Some varieties are self-fertile but all do better if they have companions, so plant two if you have the space. If you have a small garden, consider one on a dwarfing rootstock, which will only reach a height of about 3m or a fan-trained one, which will take up little space but still provide lots of tasty fruit. Keep the tree well watered until it's established and apply a thick layer of mulch in spring to help it retain precious moisture.

Fruit leathers

Making fruit leather is similar to making fruit cheese, except that once you've made your purée you bake it very slowly in the oven until it forms a pliable sheet.

For every 1kg fruit you'll need
   140g runny honey

Cook the fruit down with a little water until very soft, then press through a nylon sieve and stir in the honey while it's still warm. Line baking sheets with parchment, brush them with a little groundnut oil and spread out the purée in a thin, even layer. Bake at the lowest possible oven temperature for 6–8 hours, until pliable but not sticky. Cool and then roll it up in clingfilm or cut it into strips, roll them up and store in an airtight container.

Fruit leathers keep for 2 months in an airtight container or 4 months in the fridge.

Raspberry & scented pelargonium jam

This jam is a good way of using Scented Pelargonium Sugar (page 98), which enhances the natural sweetness of the raspberries with its own subtle aroma.

Makes approx. 6 x 220g jars.

1kg raspberries
1kg scented pelargonium sugar (page 98), sifted to
  remove any leaves
Jars

Preserving pan or large, non-reactive saucepan

Put two saucers in the freezer.

Place the raspberries in the preserving pan and mash them roughly with a wooden spoon or potato masher. Heat very gently until the fruit is just simmering, then add the sugar. Continue to cook, stirring, on a very low heat until the sugar has dissolved. Raise the temperature and boil rapidly for 10–15 minutes until the setting point is reached. You can test this by spooning a little of the jam onto one of the chilled saucers and leaving it for a moment to cool. Push it with your finger, and if it wrinkles, the jam is ready.

Remove from the heat and skim off any scum with a slotted spoon. Pot up into hot, sterilised jars and seal.

The jam will keep, sealed, for up to a year.

PACKAGING IDEA
Create an afternoon-tea basket by packing up a jar of this jam with a batch of freshly cooked scones.

PLANTING RASPBERRIES

When planning your raspberry beds, choose as sunny a spot as you can. Raspberries, *Rubus idaeus*, are self-fertile and pollinated by insects, so give them some protection in windy sites. Ideally, you want well-drained soil which has a neutral to slightly acidic pH value. A couple of weeks before planting, clear the soil of weeds, dig in some well-rotted manure and erect post-and-wire supports for the canes. Plant your raspberries in winter, in rows about 50cm apart, allowing 2m between rows. Cut the canes down to about 30cm above the soil, pruning above a bud, and water in well. Raspberries fruit on last year's canes, so you won't get any fruit in the first summer after planting.

Blackberry gin

This delicious, fruity gin can be enjoyed ice-cold in shot glasses, added to a glass of champagne or poured over ice and topped up with soda water. It makes a special gift on its own, or pair it with some pretty glasses or a bottle of fizz if you're feeling generous. Makes approx. 1.4 litres.

1kg blackberries, washed and picked over
600g golden caster sugar
1 vanilla pod, split lengthways with
 a small, sharp knife
1 litre gin
2-litre screwtop or Kilner-type jar
2 x 750ml bottles

Funnel

Make sure that the jar is scrupulously clean and add the blackberries and sugar in layers, tucking the vanilla pod somewhere in the middle. Pour over 750ml of the gin, seal the lid and shake gently. The next day, once the blackberries have settled a bit, top up with the remaining gin.

Shake the jar every day for a week to dissolve the sugar completely. Then shake once a week for about 8 weeks. Strain the liquid through a fine sieve and pour through a funnel into the bottles and seal. The boozy blackberries are delicious on ice cream, so don't discard them.

Keep the gin in a cool, dark place for 12 months before drinking if you can, though it tastes very good after as little as 3 months.

ALTERNATIVE: QUINCE VODKA

You can use the same method to make quince vodka, which takes on the deliciously perfumed flavour of the quinces and turns an elegant shade of pale amber. Simply wash any fluff from the skin of about 1kg quinces, then grate the skin and flesh (discarding any pips) and tip into a large jar, alternating layers of grated quince with 150g golden caster sugar. You could also add a couple of star anise, a cinnamon stick or a split vanilla pod to the jar before topping up with about 1½ litres vodka.

GROWING BLACKBERRIES

Gathering a basket of juicy blackberries, *Rubus fruticosus*, along the hedgerows is one of the joys of late summer. But if you have space, it's simple to establish your own patch. They're the easiest of berries to grow, tolerating fairly poor soil and some shade with fruity good humour. Many cultivated varieties have the advantage of being thornless and tend to be plumper and sweeter than wild ones too. All blackberries are self-fertile. Plant them in the autumn, digging plenty of well-rotted manure or organic matter into the planting hole, and mulch in spring. Water during dry spells in the growing season and cut back fruiting stems after harvesting to allow for new growth. Blackberries can be fan-trained up a wall or fence, which makes picking even easier.

Quince jellies

These jewel-like sweets in a rich shade of amber are a delicious way to end a meal. Take a box of them along to a dinner party as a fruity alternative to chocolates.

Makes about 40 jellies.

Approx. 1kg quinces
2 strips of lemon peel, pared
   with a sharp vegetable peeler
   and all white pith removed
Approx. 700g granulated sugar,
   plus extra for coating
   the jellies
A little vegetable oil,
   for greasing
Baking tray, approx.
   32 x 20 x 2cm

Wash the quinces to remove any of the fluffy coating on the skin. Chop roughly, without peeling or coring. Put the quinces in a large pan with the lemon zest and add just enough water to cover. Bring to a simmer and cook until soft and pulpy. Cover and leave overnight.

Rub the quinces through a sieve. Weigh the purée and return it to a large, clean pan with an equal weight of sugar. Warm gently, stirring until the sugar has dissolved. Bring to a gentle boil and cook, stirring frequently, until the mixture is thick, stiff and glossy. This can take up to 1½ hours. The jelly is ready when, if you draw a wooden spoon through the middle, the bottom of the pan is visible for a second before the mixture comes back together.

Line the baking tray with baking parchment and brush lightly with oil. Pour the mixture into the tray and leave overnight in a cool, dry place to set. Once it is set, turn the mixture out onto a sheet of baking parchment and cut into jellies. Toss in granulated sugar to coat.

Stored in an airtight container with greaseproof paper between the layers, the jellies will keep for up to a month.

GROWING QUINCES

Quince, *Cydonia oblonga*, are self-fertile and relatively low-maintenance. They make a beautiful addition to any garden and are enormously useful in the kitchen.

Plant quinces in late autumn before the first frosts in rich, moist, well-draining soil. They prefer a sunny, sheltered spot, and in cooler regions they do better fan-trained against a warm, protective, south-facing wall rather than on an open site. Trees may need staking and pruning to encourage branching in the first few years. Cut back the branch leaders to about half their length in winter; thereafter, you only need to prune dead or diseased wood. Mulch in the spring and water in dry spells. Pick fruit in autumn before the first frosts, when they have turned from green to golden and come away from the tree easily. Bring them into the house to ripen fully, at which point they will release their intoxicating perfume which will scent the whole house.

Apple water

This is a very good, light toner which balances oily skin. Makes approx. 250ml.

1 apple
70ml witch hazel
50ml cider vinegar
½ teaspoon benzoin tincture (a natural preservative)
3 drops lavender essential oil
Dark glass bottle/s

Muslin

Core the apple and discard the pips. Chop it into small pieces and place in a pan with 150ml water. Bring to the boil and simmer gently for 5–10 minutes until very soft. Remove from the heat and cool.

Place a sieve over a jug and line with muslin. Strain the apple water, then whisk in the witch hazel, vinegar and benzoin tincture. Decant into cold, sterilised glass bottles and seal.

To use the apple water, soak a cotton-wool pad with the mixture and wipe it gently all over the face and neck.

The water will keep for 2 weeks in the fridge.

ALTERNATIVE: QUINCE WATER

This is a particularly good toner for dry or mature skin. Make it in the same way as the apple water above, but don't core the quince. Simply chop up a quince, unpeeled, into small pieces and put it in a small pan; make sure you include the seeds. Add enough water to cover by a couple of centimetres. Simmer, partially covered, stirring from time to time, until the quince is very soft. Strain through a muslin-lined sieve and proceed as for the apple water. The water will keep for 2 weeks in the fridge.

GROWING APPLE AND QUINCE TREES IN POTS

If you have a small garden or terrace, it's possible to grow apple and quince trees in pots, though they will need a little more attention than those grown in the ground. Choose a tree grafted onto a dwarfing rootstock. For apples, look for M27 or M9 rootstock, for quince, try a dwarfing variety which won't grow taller than 1.3–1.5m high. Make sure you choose a self-fertile variety of apple if you only have room for one; all quinces are self-fertile. You'll need a pot around 45–60cm in diameter with holes in the base for drainage. Put a layer of crocks in the bottom and then a layer of gravel to stop the soil clogging up the drainage holes. Fill the container with soil-based compost and plant the tree. Water it in well and add a layer of mulch to help the soil retain moisture. In summer, you'll need to ensure the tree is well watered, especially during hot spells, and give it a feed with a high-potash fertiliser in late winter or early spring.

Strawberry skin cream

This intensely moisturising cream is perfect for applying to the skin after an evening bath. It contains the juice of strawberries which are high in salicylic acid, a popular ingredient in beauty treatments because of its blemish-banishing properties. Makes approx. 400g.

160ml apricot kernel, jojoba or sweet almond oil
60ml coconut or rosehip oil
25g shea butter
20g beeswax, grated
150g ripe strawberries, hulled
125ml rose water
½ teaspoon benzoin tincture (a natural preservative)
4 vitamin E capsules
2–3 jars

Bain-marie (optional)

Place the oils, shea butter and beeswax in a bain-marie or in a bowl sitting over barely simmering water – the bottom of the bowl should not touch the water. When everything has melted together, remove from the heat and leave to cool to room temperature.

Pulse the strawberries in a food processor until very smooth. Push through a sieve to remove all of the pips – you should have about 100ml of fine purée. Mix with the rose water and benzoin tincture. Pierce the vitamin E capsules with a pin and mix in their contents too.

Scrape the oil mixture into the processor and process for a minute at full speed. With the motor running, pour the strawberry mixture through the feed tube and process until you have a smooth and creamy emulsion – it's a little like making mayonnaise. Spoon into cold, sterilised jars and seal.

The cream will keep for 3 weeks in the fridge.

PACKAGING IDEA
Combining the cream with a beautiful bathrobe would make a perfect pampering gift.

GROWING STRAWBERRIES
Strawberries, *Fragaria*, love sunshine and rich soil, so choose a sunny spot and prepare the bed by digging in plenty of well-rotted manure. Place the plants about 40cm apart, in rows which are 80cm apart. When the fruits begin to appear in late spring, lay straw beneath the spreading plants to inhibit weed growth, help the soil retain moisture and stop the fruit from lying on the ground. You may also want to throw some nets over your bed to stop the birds stealing your precious fruit. The strawberry plants' yield will start to reduce after three or four years, so replace to ensure a bountiful supply.

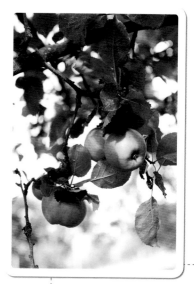

Toffee apples

For the perfect toffee apple, pick an apple with crisp flesh and some tartness to its flavour, to counterbalance the sweetness of the shiny toffee coating – Braeburn, Discovery, Cox's Orange Pippin or James Grieve all work well. Toffee apples might be a traditional autumn treat for children's parties, but don't leave them to the kids. They can also be a lighthearted, informal way to end a grown-up dinner. Makes 6.

6 apples
100g golden caster sugar
120g demerara sugar
1 teaspoon cider vinegar
2 tablespoons golden syrup
25g butter, plus a little extra for greasing

6 ice-lolly sticks or twigs
Sugar thermometer (optional)
Cellophane and ribbon, for wrapping

Rinse the apples under very hot water, then rub them dry with a clean tea towel to remove any wax coating (which can make it difficult for the toffee to stick). Press a stick into the stalk end of each apple, making sure it's firmly secured. Line a baking sheet with baking parchment and lightly butter the parchment. If you don't have a sugar thermometer, place a glass of cold water by the stove.

Place the two sugars and 100ml water in a heavy-bottomed saucepan and warm over a medium-low heat until the sugar has completely dissolved. Stir in the vinegar, golden syrup and butter. Place the sugar thermometer, if you are using one, into the pan. Bring to a rolling boil and cook, without stirring, until the toffee reaches the hard-crack stage. This is when the thermometer reads 150°C, or when a small amount of mixture dropped into the glass of water will form a hard ball. This process will take 15–20 minutes, but keep a close eye on the toffee as it can burn very quickly. Remove the pan from the heat and tilt it towards you. Swirl each apple in the toffee until it's well coated and then place on the prepared baking sheet to cool.

These toffee apples, wrapped in cellophane and tied securely with ribbon, will keep well for 2–3 days in a cool, dry place.

GROWING APPLES

Even without the enormous pleasures of its versatile fruit, it would be worth growing an apple tree for its beauty alone. Wreathed in frothy blossom in spring, heavy with apples in the autumn, *Malus domestica* earns its keep in any garden. There are thousands of varieties to choose from, so it's a good idea if possible to taste before you plant. If you have room for only one tree, make sure it is a self-fertile variety. If you are very short on space, investigate trees on a dwarfing or semi-dwarfing rootstock and those which can be espaliered or fan-trained against a wall. Plant bare-rooted varieties in a sunny, sheltered spot in late autumn or winter, when the tree is in its dormant state. Container-grown varieties can be planted year-round, but it's best to avoid planting them in the heat of the summer to give them the best opportunity to thrive.

Roast vegetable crisps

A bag of roast vegetable crisps is a great gift to take to an informal party or picnic. Makes approx. 600g.

2 beetroots, peeled
3 large carrots, peeled
3 large parsnips, peeled
3 tablespoons olive oil
Sea salt flakes
A few grinds of black pepper

Mandoline or sharp vegetable peeler

Preheat the oven to 200°C/gas mark 6. Put a couple of baking sheets in the oven to warm up.

Use a mandoline or sharp vegetable peeler to pare slices of the vegetables as thinly as possible; with the carrots and parsnips, pare them in long strips. Pat the sliced vegetables with kitchen paper or a clean tea towel to remove any moisture.

Put the beetroot in one bowl and the carrots and parsnips in another – this stops the beetroot discolouring the other vegetables. Trickle some oil, salt and pepper over the vegetables and toss them with your hands until they are thinly coated in the oil.

Remove the hot trays from the oven and quickly arrange the vegetable slices on them in a single layer (you may need to bake the crisps in batches). Put them in the oven and cook for 15–20 minutes, turning them over half-way through, until the edges are crisp and they are beginning to curl. Season with a little more salt while still warm. Place the baking sheets on wire racks to cool. When the crisps are completely cold, store them in an airtight container or bag.

The crisps will keep in an airtight container for 3–4 days.

PACKAGING IDEA

Decorate paper bags to hold your crisps with simple vegetable stamps. To create the easiest stamp of all, cut a small beetroot in half and hold it down firmly on a paper bag for a couple of seconds. The natural dye in the beetroot makes an attractive, distinctive stamp.

GROWING BEETROOT

Prepare your vegetable bed by making sure it's free of weeds and large stones. If possible, dig some well-rotted compost into the bed the autumn before planting. Sow beetroot, *Beta vulgaris*, seeds directly into the ground from late spring to summer, as successive plantings every month or so will ensure a continuous supply. Sow the seeds at a depth of 2cm in rows 25cm apart, then rake the soil back over the seeds. Once the seeds are large enough to handle, begin thinning them out to about 10cm apart. Water well during dry spells and keep the plot weed-free while the plants establish themselves. Harvest your beetroot when they're about the size of golf balls to enjoy them at their sweetest. One of the advantages of growing your own beetroot is that you get to enjoy the leaves too, which are so often lopped off when you buy them. Use the young leaves as you would spinach in salads and soups.

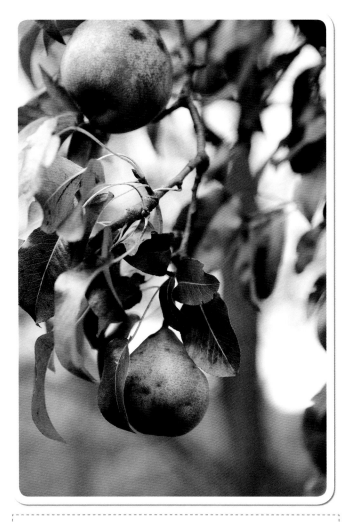

Spiced pear crisps

One of the great autumn quests is seeking out the perfectly ripe pear. If you have lots of hard fruit, however, use them to make these spiced pear crisps. More chewy than crisp, they're a welcome present to take along on an autumnal walk. Makes approx. 50–60 crisps.

4 very firm pears
Juice of 1 lemon

4 tablespoons golden caster sugar
¾ teaspoon ground cinnamon
½ teaspoon ground ginger
¼ teaspoon grated nutmeg
Pinch of ground cloves

Mandoline
Silpat sheets or oven-proof wire racks

Preheat the oven to 130°C/gas mark 1.

Halve each pear, remove the stem and use a teaspoon to scoop out the core. Slice thinly using the mandoline, then place the slices in a large bowl, tossing them in the lemon juice as you go. Drain them in a colander and pat dry with kitchen paper or a clean tea towel. Lay the slices on a wire rack placed over a tray.

In a small bowl, combine the sugar and spices. Sift a fine dusting of the mixture over the pears, turn them over and coat the other side.

Line two large baking trays with Silpat. If you don't have Silpat sheets, place oven-proof wire racks over the baking trays and put sheets of baking parchment on top. Place the pears on the Silpat or baking parchment and bake for about 1 hour 15 minutes, turning over once or twice. The cooking time will depend on how thin the slices are and you may need to extend it slightly. Cool the pears on wire racks. When completely cold, store in an airtight container.

The pear crisps will keep for 3–4 days.

GROWING PEARS

Give pear trees, *Pyrus communis*, a sunny, sheltered location with well-drained soil away from frost pockets. As the trees establish, water them well during dry periods, particularly once the fruit starts to swell, and mulch around the base with well-rotted manure in early spring. Some pears are self-fertile, but all fruit better with a companion. Ask the nursery about pollination groups as not all are compatible. For a small garden, consider trees on a dwarfing rootstock. Some varieties also do well as cordons, fans or espaliers.

GROWING TOMATOES

It's easy to find small tomato plants in garden centres but you will have a far wider, more interesting choice if you grow them from seed. In early spring, sow seeds in seed trays or small pots, cover them with plastic bags and place on a sunny window sill to germinate. Transfer to 9cm pots once two true leaves have formed. When the flowers on the first truss begin to open, harden them off for several days if you're going to grow them outdoors, then transfer them to 23cm pots, grow bags or plant them in the ground about 50cm apart. If you're growing them in the garden rather than under glass, select a sheltered spot with as much direct sun as you can and dig some well-rotted manure into the soil a couple of weeks before you plant them out. Feed them every couple of weeks with high-potash tomato feed when they start to flower and tie cordon varieties into canes for support. Pinch out shoots which develop between the stem and main branches and water regularly and frequently to prevent the skins of the fruit splitting.

Tomato ketchup

This is a great way to make use of a glut of tomatoes. For the best flavour, it's essential that you choose very ripe fruit. Makes about 1.5 litres.

3kg very ripe tomatoes, roughly chopped
1 onion, finely diced
200ml cider vinegar
120g light muscovado sugar
3 garlic cloves, chopped
1 teaspoon paprika
1 teaspoon salt
½ teaspoon English mustard powder
Bottles with vinegar-proof lids

FOR THE PICKLING SPICES:

1 teaspoon black or white peppercorns
½ teaspoon allspice berries
½ teaspoon whole cloves
2.5cm piece of fresh ginger, peeled and sliced
1 small bay leaf
1 blade of mace
½ cinnamon stick

Muslin
Kitchen string
Preserving pan or large, non-reactive pan
Nylon sieve

Tie up the pickling spices in a circle of muslin with kitchen string. Put the spice bag into a preserving pan or large, non-reactive saucepan with all the other ingredients. Cook over a low heat until the tomatoes are pulpy and all of the sugar is dissolved, then raise the heat and simmer, stirring from time to time, for about 2 hours until the mixture has reduced and thickened. Remove the spice bag.

Place a nylon sieve over a large bowl and press the mixture through the sieve. Return it to the cleaned pan, taste and add more sugar if necessary (the amount of sugar needed depends on how ripe and sweet the tomatoes are). Simmer the sauce for 5 minutes, or until it has the thickness you like. Decant through a funnel into hot, sterilised bottles and seal. Store in a cool, dark place for 2 weeks before using. The ketchup will keep for 3 months, unopened, in a cool, dark place. After opening, refrigerate and use within a week.

Green tomato chutney

When the days grow shorter and an autumn chill creeps into the air, making green tomato chutney is a wonderful way to use up those tomatoes which will never ripen. For perfect texture, it's worth the effort of ensuring the vegetables are cut into even-sized chunks. Makes approx. 10 x 220ml jars.

1kg green tomatoes, diced
400g onions, finely chopped
1 tablespoon sea salt flakes
400g cooking apples, peeled
   and cored weight, diced
3 yellow peppers, cored
   and diced
3 garlic cloves, minced
350g light muscovado sugar
400ml cider vinegar
½ teaspoon chilli flakes
Jars with vinegar-proof lids

FOR THE SPICE BAG
25g piece of fresh ginger,
   peeled and sliced
1 teaspoon coriander seeds
1 teaspoon black peppercorns
1 teaspoon mustard seeds
3 cloves
1 star anise

Preserving pan or other large,
   non-reactive saucepan
Muslin
Kitchen string

Green tomatoes, because they are unripe, can take a long time to soften in cooking. Layering them beforehand in a large pan with the onions, sprinkling a little salt between each layer, and leaving overnight, will soften them and therefore shorten the cooking time.

Tie the spices into a small square of muslin with kitchen string and place in the pan with the tomatoes, onions and all the rest of the ingredients. Stir over a low heat, without boiling, until the sugar has dissolved. Bring to the boil and cook, uncovered, stirring from time to time to make sure nothing is sticking, until the chutney is thick and glossy. When you draw a wooden spoon through the middle of the pan, it should leave the bottom of the pan visible for a second or two before the mixture comes back together. This will take about 1–1½ hours.

Remove the spice bag and ladle the chutney into warm, sterilised jars. Seal with vinegar-proof lids and leave for at least 6 weeks before eating.

The chutney will keep in a cool, dark place for up to 2 years.

PACKAGING IDEA
A jar of this chutney with a wedge of strong, hard cheese, such as a mature Cheddar, and a box of oatcakes makes a great gift. Add a cheese knife too, to make it into a more substantial present.

GROWING GARLIC
Garlic, *Allium sativum*, is pleasingly uncomplicated to grow. Traditionally, it was planted on the shortest day of the year, but somewhere between the first and the last winter frost will do. Plant garlic in a sunny position, in free-draining soil. Break the bulb into cloves and plant them about 10cm apart, pushing them down so the tip is about 3cm below the surface. Alternatively, you can grow them in containers; about four cloves to a 16–20cm pot. Keep well weeded and water well in dry periods to ensure fat, juicy bulbs. Harvest the bulbs in late summer when the leaves turn yellow. In sunny weather you can leave them hanging outside to dry; alternatively, hang them in a cool, dry and well-ventilated place indoors. They should take about 3–4 weeks to dry fully.

Seasoned olives

Next time you're invited to a dinner party, take along a couple of jars of these seasoned olives as a tasty alternative to a bunch of flowers. Makes 2 x 500g jars.

SEASONING FOR BLACK OLIVES

150ml olive oil

6 garlic cloves, bashed

1 bay leaf

1 tablespoon finely chopped rosemary

Thinly pared zest of 1 lemon, all traces of white pith removed

350g black olives cured in brine, rinsed

SEASONING FOR GREEN OLIVES

150ml olive oil

Thinly pared zest of 1 orange

4 tablespoons finely chopped coriander

½ teaspoon coriander seeds, roughly crushed in a pestle and mortar

¼ teaspoon chilli flakes

350g green olives cured in brine, rinsed

2 jars

To make the black olive seasoning, pour the oil into a small pan with the garlic and warm over a low heat until bubbles appear around the edge of the pan. Poach the garlic in the oil for 5 minutes, then remove from the heat. When the oil is cold, toss it with the rest of the ingredients, including the olives. Spoon into an airtight jar and refrigerate.

To make the green olive blend, simply mix all of the ingredients together, seal in a jar and refrigerate.

The olives will keep, refrigerated, for up to 5 days. Bring to room temperature before eating.

PACKAGING IDEA If you're feeling generous, pack a pair of olive bowls into a box alongside the jars.

GROWING CORIANDER

Coriander (*Coriandrum sativum*) is a tender annual best grown in light soil where it can enjoy a little shade during the hottest part of the day. Sow it directly into the ground in late spring in 1cm drills and cover lightly with soil. Thin out to about 10cm apart once the seedlings are large enough to handle. Staggered planting throughout the summer will ensure a plentiful supply of fresh leaves. Don't overwater coriander as it hates to be soggy, but don't let it dry out either as that will encourage its propensity to bolt. Do let some go to seed, however. Once the seeds ripen and start to become fragrant, harvest them as described on page 19.

Courgette & ricotta muffins

A basket of muffins is always a welcome gift. These light and tender savoury ones are a delicious way of using up a plentiful crop of courgettes in summer. Alternatively, use grated carrot instead of courgettes and Cheddar in place of the Parmesan. Makes 12.

240g plain flour
2 teaspoons baking powder
½ teaspoon bicarbonate of soda
½ teaspoon salt
A few grinds of black pepper
1 teaspoon finely chopped fresh oregano or marjoram
120g Parmesan, coarsely grated
2 free-range eggs, lightly beaten
200g ricotta
100ml olive oil
200g courgettes, coarsely grated
5 spring onions, finely chopped
Paper cases

Muffin tin

Preheat the oven to 200°C/gas mark 6 and line a muffin tin with 12 paper cases.

Sift together the flour, baking powder and bicarbonate of soda. Whisk in the salt, pepper, oregano or marjoram and 80g of the Parmesan.

In a separate bowl, whisk together the eggs, ricotta and olive oil. Fold this into the flour with a spatula until just combined – be careful not to overmix as it will make the muffins tough. Fold in the courgettes and spring onions.

Spoon the batter into the paper cases and sprinkle over the rest of the Parmesan. Bake for 18–20 minutes, until a toothpick inserted into the middle of a muffin comes out clean.

These muffins are best eaten on the day of baking, though they freeze quite well.

GROWING COURGETTES

Courgettes, *Cucurbita pepa*, are possibly the easiest of all vegetables to grow. Sow seeds singly in small pots indoors in spring and harden them off by placing them outside in a sheltered spot during the day and then bringing them in at night for about a week. Only plant them out once all threat of frost has passed. Plant them in the ground about 1m apart, or grow them in pots at least 40cm in diameter. Keep courgettes well watered and pick them when they're no larger than 10cm long for the best flavour. One of the benefits of growing your own courgettes is that you get to harvest the beautiful yellow flowers. You can eat them fresh or stuff them with soft goat's cheese, dip them in a light tempura batter and deep-fry them until golden.

Mushroom ketchup

This intensely savoury condiment has been enjoyed in England for centuries, far longer than the Johnny-come-lately tomato version. It's great for adding a kick to all manner of dishes, from shepherd's pie to gravies, soups and stews. It's the secret, savoury weapon in many a dedicated cook's culinary arsenal. Makes approx. 700ml.

1.2kg mushrooms, sliced
3 tablespoons sea salt flakes
50g dried porcini mushrooms
200ml red wine vinegar
4 shallots, very finely diced
2 tablespoons light muscovado
 sugar

FOR THE SPICE MIXTURE
2.5cm piece of fresh ginger, peeled
 and thinly sliced
1 small bay leaf
1 teaspoon black peppercorns
½ teaspoon allspice berries
½ teaspoon whole cloves
¼ teaspoon freshly grated nutmeg

Bottles with vinegar-proof lids

Muslin
Kitchen string
Preserving pan or large,
 non-reactive saucepan
Funnel

Layer the mushrooms in a non-reactive bowl, sprinkling salt between each layer and then on top. Cover with clingfilm and leave in a cool place for 24 hours, stirring and pressing down on the mushrooms with a wooden spoon a couple of times as they macerate.

When you're ready to make the ketchup, put the dried porcini into a small bowl and pour over 250ml boiling water. Leave to soak for an hour, then scoop them out with a slotted spoon. Line a sieve with muslin and pour the soaking liquid through it into a jug to remove any grit.

Tie the spice mixture into a circle of muslin with kitchen string.

Put the sliced mushrooms and any liquid from their bowl into the pan. Add the dried mushrooms, their soaking liquid and the rest of the ingredients, including the spice bag. Bring to the boil, lower the temperature and simmer for about 1½ hours, stirring from time to time, until the mixture is very thick.

Remove the spice bag and blitz the mushrooms in a food processor or blender until very smooth. You may have to do this in batches. Return to the cleaned pan, bring to the boil and simmer for 5 minutes. Pour through a funnel into warm, sterilised bottles and seal. Allow to mature for a week before using.

The ketchup will keep for 3 months, unopened, in a cool, dark place. After opening, refrigerate and use within a week.

GROWING MUSHROOMS
Many people, quite rightly, are nervous about gathering wild mushrooms. If you're not absolutely sure of what you're doing, the consequences can be fatal. But by growing your own you have the pleasure of gathering mushrooms without the fear.

Mushroom-growing kits come in a wide range of varieties, from shiitake, to oyster, chestnut, chicken of the woods and portobello, to name but some of the more readily available ones. Generally, they come in two forms: plugs which you insert into holes drilled into hardwood logs or complete kits which include grow boxes and mushroom culture pre-sown with spawn. Simply follow the supplier's cultivation instructions for each variety.

PACKAGING IDEA
Growing mushrooms is a compelling hobby and one that children often enjoy too, so pack a mushroom-growing kit with the bottle of ketchup.

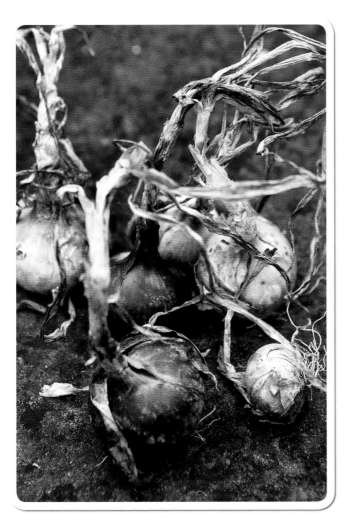

Onion marmalade

This marmalade is a fantastic accompaniment to cold meats, strong cheeses and pâtés. It makes a very good Christmas present. Makes 6 x 220g jars.

80g unsalted butter
2 tablespoons olive oil
2kg onions, halved and finely sliced
2 sprigs of thyme
1 bay leaf
1 teaspoon salt
250g caster sugar
250ml cider vinegar
100ml red wine
Black pepper
Jars with vinegar-proof lids

Preserving pan or large, non-reactive saucepan

Heat the butter and oil in a large saucepan over a medium-low heat. When the butter stops foaming, add the onions, thyme, bay leaf and salt. Cook gently, stirring from time to time, until the onions are very soft and a pale golden colour. This will take 45 minutes to an hour. Remove the bay leaf and thyme.

Raise the heat a little, add the sugar and continue to cook, stirring frequently, until the mixture is a deep shade of golden amber. Remove from the heat, add the vinegar, wine and a few grinds of black pepper and give everything a good stir. Return the pan to the stove and cook fairly briskly for 30 minutes, stirring regularly, until thickened and rich.

Spoon the marmalade into warm, sterilised jars and seal with vinegar-proof lids.

The marmalade will keep for 6 months, unopened, in a cool, dark place. After opening, refrigerate and use within a week.

GROWING ONIONS

Choose a sunny, sheltered, well-drained site for your onions, *Allium cepa*, and, a few months before you want to plant them, dig the patch over, removing any stones and working in some well-rotted manure. In spring, buy immature onions, called sets, from garden centres. Plant them 10–15cm apart in shallow drills and cover them so the tips are only just protruding from the soil. Keep the site as weed-free as possible and water during dry weather. Stop watering once the onions have swollen and in late summer scrape away any soil around the bulbs so they're exposed to the sun. When the foliage turns yellow, the onions are ready to harvest. Lift them and leave them to dry for a few days in the sun, or in a shed if the weather is wet.

Chilli vodka

Fiery chilli vodka adds a pleasing kick to a bloody mary or is delicious on its own served ice-cold in shot glasses. Makes 750ml.

2–3 hot chillies such as jalapeños, habaneros or Hungarian hot wax, washed, plus 1–2 extra for finishing the bottle
¼ teaspoon peppercorns (optional)
750ml bottle vodka

1-litre jar
750ml bottle (use the bottle the vodka came in if you like)

Funnel

Having first removed the green calyx, slice each chilli in half lengthways. Tip them into a cold, sterilised 1-litre jar, with the peppercorns, if you're using them, and pour over the vodka. Seal the jar and leave in a cool, dark place for 2 weeks.

Strain the vodka into a jug. Drop the extra chilli/es into a cold, sterilised 750ml bottle and pour the vodka in through a funnel. Seal and chill before serving.

The vodka will keep well for at least 6 months.

PACKAGING IDEA

If you're feeling generous, a pretty glass pitcher and some shot glasses make a great addition to the bottle of vodka.

GROWING CHILLIES

Chillies are the fiery members of the capsicum family. Growing them is enormously rewarding, not just because of their myriad culinary uses but also because they make dramatically beautiful plants. Start seedlings off indoors and move them to a sunny spot outside in late spring when all threat of frost has passed. Chillies do very well in pots, either on a sunny window sill or on a sheltered terrace. You will need to stake them when they reach about 20cm and pinch out the first flowers before they set fruit in order to encourage bushy growth. Ensure that the compost doesn't dry out in hot weather, as chillies are quite thirsty, and feed them weekly after the first flowers appear with a high-potash liquid feed. Pick them as you need them, from high summer through to autumn. Towards the end of the season, you can dry any which remain on the plant in an airing cupboard or in the oven on its lowest setting for around 4 hours or so.

Chilli jam

This fiery preserve goes wonderfully with strong, hard cheeses, sausages and grilled meats. Take it along as a gift to a barbecue where not only can it be served as a condiment, but it can be also thinned with a little boiling water and used as a glaze for pieces of chicken or lamb chops. The number of chillies you use will depend on their heat and how hot you want the jam to be. Makes approx. 5 x 220g jars.

1.5kg very ripe tomatoes, peeled and
    roughly chopped
900g caster sugar
250ml red wine vinegar
5cm piece of fresh ginger, peeled
    and grated
4–6 red chillies, halved, membranes and
    seeds removed and finely sliced
6 garlic cloves, finely minced
1 star anise (optional)
1 teaspoon salt
Jars with
    vinegar-
    proof lids

Preserving pan
    or large, non-
    reactive saucepan

Place all the ingredients in the preserving pan and warm over a medium heat, stirring, until the sugar has dissolved. Bring to the boil, then reduce the heat and simmer, stirring from time to time, for 35–45 minutes, until the mixture has thickened and reduced to a jammy consistency. Remove the star anise.

Spoon into warm, sterilised jars and seal with vinegar-proof lids.

The jam will keep for a month, unopened, in a cool, dark place. After opening, refrigerate and use within a week.

TYPES OF CHILLIES TO GROW

There are so many different kinds of chillies, with different degrees of heat, it can be tricky to choose just a few. Here are some great varieties to get you started.

CHERRY BOMB MEDIUM hot and fruity, this is a great chilli for sprinkling on pizza, stirring into salsas or using in fiery pasta dishes.

HUNGARIAN HOT WAX despite its name, this is a mild- to medium-hot chilli. Use it while it's mild and green or wait for it to become ripe and red if you like a little more heat. This is a very good all-round chilli and one of the easiest to grow.

JALAPEÑO this chilli ripens from green to red, though it is almost always used green. It's a very good chilli for pickling, adding to salsas or stuffing with cheese and roasting.

NUMEX TWILIGHT this hot chilli is almost worth growing for its beauty alone. The plant displays fruits at all stages of ripeness, so it's covered in purple, yellow, orange and red chillies all at the same time. For information on growing chillies, see page 157.

Seedy crackers

These crackers are simple to make and rival anything from an upmarket deli. The dough freezes well so make a couple of batches and keep one in the freezer for when you need to rustle up a gift at short notice. Makes approx. 30.

180g plain flour
80g spelt flour
1 teaspoon baking powder
2 tablespoons celery seeds
2 tablespoons fennel seeds
1 tablespoon caraway seeds
½ teaspoon freshly ground
   black pepper
½ teaspoon sea salt flakes
70g unsalted butter, chilled and
   cut into small chunks

Preheat the oven to 180°C/gas mark 4. Line two baking sheets with baking parchment.

Sift the flours and baking powder into a bowl. Whisk in the salt. Add the butter and rub in with your fingertips until the mixture resembles fine breadcrumbs. Mix in the seeds and pepper.

Make a well in the centre and slowly add 120–140ml iced water, cutting it in with a knife to blend, then kneading it lightly with your hands until you have a firm dough. Cut the dough in half, wrap in clingfilm and refrigerate for 15 minutes.

Remove one piece of dough from the fridge. Place between two pieces of clingfilm and roll out to 3mm thick. Dip a 5cm round cutter in flour and cut out the crackers. Place them on the prepared baking sheet. Repeat with the other half of the dough, then refrigerate both lots for 30 minutes.

Bake for 25–30 minutes until the crackers are just turning golden. Cool on the tray for 5 minutes, then place on a wire rack to cool completely.

The crackers will keep in an airtight container for 4–5 days.

PACKAGING IDEA

A box of these crackers with a great piece of strong Cheddar and a jar of Green Tomato Chutney (page 148) would make an excellent gift.

GROWING CELERY

Celery, *Apium graveolens*, is such an essential ingredient to so many soups and casseroles it's surprising more of us don't grow it, particularly as there are new, self-blanching varieties. Prepare the bed in a sunny spot a couple of months before you want to plant them out, as for onions (page 155). Sow seeds inside in spring in seed trays or modules and cover with a fine layer of vermiculite. When large enough to handle, move them into 7.5cm pots. Then in early summer, when the plants are about 10cm high, harden them off for a few days before planting them out about 25cm apart. Keep them well-watered. Harvest in late summer or early autumn, though leave one or two in the ground so that you can collect the seed. Celery is a biennial. Pick the stalks when they begin to dry out and lay them out on a sheet in a warm room to finish ripening. Hold the seed heads over a bowl and break them open, collecting the seeds in the bowl. Store the seeds in an airtight jar.

Pickled walnuts

If you have a walnut tree in your garden or growing wild on public land near you, gather the green walnuts in summer to create this most traditional and delicious of treats. A jar makes a wonderful Christmas present – pickled walnuts are a great addition to the cheese board or to platters of charcuterie. Makes approx. 2kg.

2kg green walnuts
Approx. 300g salt
Large jars with vinegar-proof lids

FOR THE PICKLING MIXTURE

1 teaspoon allspice berries
½ cinnamon stick
½ teaspoon black or white
   peppercorns
1 small piece of dried ginger or
   1 tablespoon grated
   fresh ginger
1 bay leaf
1 litre white wine vinegar
300g light muscovado sugar

Rubber gloves
Muslin
Kitchen string
Preserving pan or large,
   non-reactive saucepan

You need to gather the immature, green walnuts before the shells have formed. Push a thin skewer or needle into the opposite end of the walnuts from the stalk and you will be able to feel if a shell is forming beneath the green outer covering. Wear rubber gloves to handle the walnuts as they stain the hands quite dramatically and stubbornly. Prick them all over with a fork or needle.

Make a brine by dissolving salt in water in a ratio of 100g salt to 1 litre water. Soak the walnuts in the brine for a week; place a plate on top to keep the nuts submerged. Drain in a colander and repeat for a further week in a fresh brine mixture.

Drain the walnuts. Place on racks lined with baking parchment in a dry, airy and, if possible, sunny place for 2–3 days until they turn black.

Place all of the spices for the pickling mixture in a circle of muslin and tie into a bundle with kitchen string. Place the spice bundle in a large, non-reactive pan with the vinegar and sugar. Heat, stirring to dissolve the sugar, then bring to the boil. Simmer very gently for 15 minutes and discard the spice bag. Pack the walnuts into cold, sterilised jars, pour over enough of the hot spiced vinegar to cover, seal and store in a cool, dark place for 2 months before eating.

The walnuts will keep, unopened, for up to 2 years.

PACKAGING IDEA Pickled walnuts make a good companion to strong cheeses, potted meats and salamis, so pack up a jar in a small, luxuriously epicurean hamper.

PLANTING A WALNUT TREE

If you have the space, a walnut tree, *Juglans regia*, is a majestic addition to any garden. Plant in autumn or winter in fertile, free-draining soil and provide some shelter from the wind during the early years of the tree's development, though to fruit generously it will need full sun once it becomes established. Water well during hot weather in the early years to help the tree establish, and mulch around the base of the tree to keep the soil moist. Some walnuts are partially self-fertile, but all do better if cross-pollinated, so, if possible, plant near other walnut trees.

Pickled cucumbers

If you're going to a summer barbecue, take along a jar of these sour, spicy pickles. They're the perfect condiment to add to juicy burgers. Makes approx. 1kg.

1kg cucumbers, sliced
1 small onion, halved and sliced
2 tablespoons sea salt flakes
1 or 2 jars with vinegar-proof lids

FOR THE PICKLING LIQUID

500ml cider vinegar or white wine vinegar
60g caster sugar
1 teaspoon mustard seeds
6 black peppercorns
3 allspice berries
3 garlic cloves, thinly sliced

Preserving pan or large, non-reactive saucepan

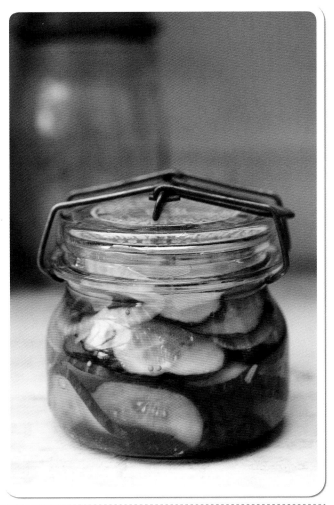

Place the cucumbers and onion in a large bowl, sprinkle over the salt and toss with your hands. Cover and leave for 2–3 hours. Drain, rinse under the cold tap and gently pat dry on a clean tea towel.

Put all of the ingredients for the pickling liquid into a non-reactive pan with 600ml water and warm gently over a low heat, stirring until the sugar has dissolved. Remove from the heat and cool.

Pack the cucumbers and onions into cold, sterilised jars. Pour over the cold pickling liquid to cover completely and seal with vinegar-proof lids. Leave for 2 days for the flavours to mellow before eating.

They will keep, sealed, in the fridge for 1 month.

GROWING CUCUMBERS OUTDOORS

Cucumbers, *Cucumis sativus*, love heat but if you don't have a heated greenhouse, try varieties such as 'Gracius', 'Marketmore' and 'Burpless Tasty Green', which do quite well out of doors. Start your seeds off indoors in mid-spring in 7.5cm pots filled with seed compost. Make a 2cm hole in the compost with a dibber/pencil and drop 2 seeds in the hole, cover with soil then water. When the seedlings are 2cm high, remove the weakest one. Harden them off for a few days before planting out in early summer in a sunny, sheltered spot, about 50cm apart. Support with canes. Water in well and feed with a high-potash fertiliser once fruit starts to appear. Pick before they get too large.

Fennel & honey face mask

Fennel is a natural astringent. It cleanses the skin and reduces puffiness. In India, gram or chickpea flour is used in many natural beauty treatments as it helps draw impurities out of the skin and is a gentle exfoliant. You can buy it from Asian stores and some supermarkets.

Makes approx. 170g, enough for 4–5 applications.

3 tablespoons fennel seeds,
   roughly crushed in a pestle and mortar
100g gram or chickpea flour
4 tablespoons runny honey
½ teaspoon benzoin tincture
   (a natural preservative)

1 jar or pot

Place the fennel seeds in a small pan with 80ml water. Bring to a simmer and immediately remove from the heat. Let the mixture cool and infuse, then strain through a fine sieve. Whisk together with the gram flour, honey and benzoin tincture until you have a thick paste. Spoon into the cold, sterilised jar or pot and seal.

The face mask should be smoothed onto a clean face and neck, left for 15 minutes, rubbed gently into the skin, then wiped off with a facecloth soaked in warm water. Rinse the skin in tepid water and pat dry with a fluffy towel before moisturising.

The face mask will keep in the fridge for 2 weeks.

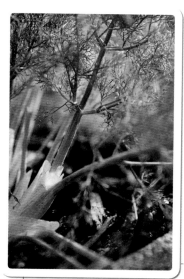

GROWING FENNEL

Airy fronds of fennel swaying in the breeze are such a pretty sight, and undoubtedly earn *Foeniculum vulgare* a place in the flower border, let alone the herb bed. Fennel can grow up to 1.5m tall and prefers rich, well-drained soil in a sunny site, though it will tolerate less-than-perfect conditions with fairly good heart. During the summer, keep picking at the fronds to encourage lots of sweet, young leaves. *F. v.* 'Purpureum', or bronze fennel, is less vigorous and has a milder flavour but is equally beautiful. The ripening seeds take on a yellowish shade. Harvest them as described on page 19.

PACKAGING IDEA Tuck a soft, pretty facecloth into the package with the jar or pot for a simple, inexpensive but nonetheless thoughtful gift. Include a card with instructions for how to use the face mask too.

Cucumber night cream

Cucumbers are intensely hydrating and nourishing. Combined with orange blossom water and neroli oil, the essential oil of the bitter orange tree which is believed to improve blood circulation and relieve anxiety, they make a rich night cream which relaxes as it moisturises. Makes approx. 4 x 100g jars.

250ml coconut oil
2 tablespoons white beeswax, grated
1 tablespoon shea butter
½ small cucumber, peeled, halved, deseeded and cut into chunks
60ml orange blossom water
¼ teaspoon benzoin tincture (a natural preservative)
4 drops neroli essential oil
Dark glass jars

Muslin

Place a small heatproof bowl over a pan of barely simmering water; the bottom of the bowl should not touch the water. Put the coconut oil in the bowl with the wax and shea butter. Warm, stirring from time to time, until the wax has melted. Remove the bowl from the heat and cool to room temperature.

While the oil is cooling, tip the cucumber into a blender or food processor and blitz until very smooth. Place a sieve over a jug and line with muslin. Pass the cucumber through the sieve, pressing down with a spatula to extract as much liquid as possible. Measure 60ml of the cucumber liquid and mix with the orange blossom water, benzoin tincture and neroli oil.

Spoon the oil mixture into the cleaned food processor or blender and process for a minute. With the motor still running, pour the cucumber mixture through the feed tube and process until you have a smooth emulsion. Use a spatula to transfer the cream into cold, sterilised jars and seal.

The cream will keep in the fridge for about 10 days.

GROWING CUCUMBERS INDOORS

If you have a heated greenhouse, you can get your crop of cucumbers going sooner than those intended for outdoors. Sow seeds in early spring, as for outdoor cucumbers (page 161).

In late spring, transfer your plants to 25cm pots or grow bags, two per bag. Keep the plants moist with regular watering and feed them with a dilute high-potash feed every two weeks or so. Train your cucumbers up canes or vertical wires for support. Once the main stem has reached the roof of the greenhouse, pinch out the growing point and the tips of the side shoots. Some cucumbers have male and female flowers on the same plant. With outdoor cucumbers, you can simply ignore these. With indoor ones, pinch out the male flowers as they appear. If they are left to develop, your cucumbers will be bitter. To tell male and female flowers apart, look for the swellings beneath the female flowers which will eventually become cucumbers.

Gentle lettuce cleanser

This is a very good, mild cleanser for dry or irritated skin. It's particularly soothing on sunburn, so it would make a thoughtful gift for anyone who's been a little casual with the sunscreen.

Makes approx. 400ml.

1 small, soft-leafed lettuce
15g young borage leaves
400ml distilled water
¼ teaspoon benzoin tincture
(a natural preservative)
2 x 200ml dark glass bottles

Muslin
Funnel

Tear the lettuce into small pieces and place in a pan with the borage and distilled water. Bring to the boil, immediately lower the temperature and simmer very gently, partially covered, for 30 minutes. Remove from the heat and cool. Line a sieve with muslin and strain the liquid into a jug. Whisk in the benzoin tincture. Decant into cold, sterilised bottles and seal.

The cleanser will keep for 2 weeks in the fridge.

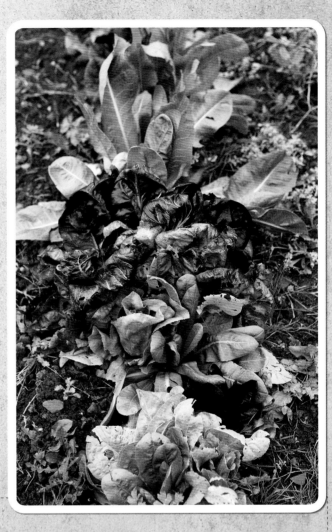

GROWING LETTUCE

What could be simpler to grow, and more delicious, than your own lettuce? With a little planning, you can have fresh leaves for most months of the year. Sow *Lactuca sativa* seeds every couple of weeks from spring until late summer to ensure a continuous supply. Plant the seeds about 1cm deep in fertile, well-drained soil in a spot where they'll have some shade from the midday sun. Thin out seedlings once the first true leaves appear so that they're about 30cm apart. Of course, you can add the thinnings to salads, so nothing is wasted. Loose-leaf varieties are among the least demanding types to grow, which is fortunate as not only are they delicious, but they're also the sort of lettuce you need to make this cleanser. Cut-and-come again varieties also grow very well in containers. All lettuce likes water, so be careful not to let the soil dry out.

Creamed horseradish

Creamed horseradish goes beautifully, of course, with roast beef and so makes a great homemade gift to take along to a Sunday lunch. Makes 2 x 150g jars.

100g crème fraîche
100ml double cream, lightly whipped
100g fresh horseradish root,
    finely grated
Pinch of sugar
Salt and freshly ground white pepper
    2 jars

Gently fold together the crème fraîche and cream until well combined. Stir in the horseradish and sugar and season to taste with salt and pepper.

Seal in cold, sterilised jars and refrigerate until ready to use.

Creamed horseradish will keep, refrigerated, for 2 days.

Pickled horseradish

Slivers of pickled horseradish add a fiery bite to many dishes, with a flavour reminiscent of Chinese pickled ginger. They can be eaten as an accompaniment to mackerel, smoked salmon or strong, hard cheeses. Makes 2 x 220g jars.

400g fresh horseradish root, peeled
    and thinly sliced with a sharp knife
    or mandoline
2 tablespoons sea salt flakes
200ml rice vinegar or cider vinegar
3 tablespoons golden caster sugar
Juice and finely grated zest of 1 lime
Juice and finely grated zest of 1 lemon
Juice and finely grated zest of
    ½ small orange
2 jars with vinegar-proof lids

Preserving pan or large,
    non-reactive saucepan

Place the horseradish in a bowl with the salt and stir to combine. Cover and leave for 12 hours or overnight, stirring once or twice. Place the horseradish in a colander and rinse briefly under cold water. Leave to drain for 15 minutes, then pat dry with a clean tea towel.

Warm the vinegar, sugar and 150ml water in a pan until simmering, stirring to dissolve the sugar. Add the lime, lemon and orange juices and zests and remove from the heat immediately.

Divide the horseradish between the two sterilised jars and pour the vinegar mixture over to cover. Seal, cool and refrigerate for a minimum of 7 days for the flavours to develop.

Refrigerated, this will keep for 1 month.

GROWING HORSERADISH

In many regions, horseradish, *Amoracia rusticana*, grows in abundance along the roadside, but make sure you get permission from the landowner before you dig it up. It is, however, very easy to grow your own. Some may say too easy: horseradish is an invasive perennial, so be careful where you place your plant. It will tolerate all kinds of soils but doesn't like heavy shade, so choose a sunny spot. In spring, take a live root about 25cm long and plant it in a hole at a depth of about 15cm, allowing about 50cm between plants. To contain its growth, horseradish can also be grown in large, deep planters such as half-barrels.

Lift horseradish roots as you need them in the autumn. To store roots over the winter, when the ground is too cold to dig them up, lift a few roots and store them in a cool, dark place in a box of dry sand.

PACKAGING IDEA

Combined with a jar of Pickled Cucumbers (page 161) or Green Tomato Chutney (page 148), either of these preserves make a great addition to a savoury hamper.

Carrot cake

Next time you're asked to bring along a cake to a party, try this moist carrot cake fragrant with spices and covered with tangy cream cheese icing.

Makes 9 squares or 1 round 22cm cake.

1 cooking apple, about 250g, peeled, cored and diced
Grated zest and juice of 1 small orange
100g sultanas or raisins
200g self-raising flour
2 teaspoons baking powder
1 teaspoon ground cinnamon
1 teaspoon ground ginger
½ teaspoon grated nutmeg
½ teaspoon salt
150g butter, melted, plus extra for greasing
3 free-range eggs
150g light muscovado sugar
240g carrots, peeled and coarsely grated
80g pecans or walnuts, toasted and roughly chopped, plus 9 whole ones to decorate

FOR THE ICING

60g unsalted butter, at room temperature
240g cream cheese, at room temperature
1 teaspoon lemon juice
Finely grated zest of 1 small lemon
240g icing sugar, sifted

20 x 20 x 8cm square cake tin or a 22cm loose-bottomed cake tin

Preheat the oven to 170°C/gas mark 3. Grease the cake tin and line the bottom and sides with baking parchment. Butter the parchment.

Put the apple into a small pan with the orange juice and the sultanas or raisins. Cook gently until the apples are soft and pulpy. Leave to cool.

Sift together the flour, baking powder, cinnamon, ginger, nutmeg and salt.

In a separate bowl, whisk together the butter, eggs and sugar until they are very light and foamy. Gently fold in the flour until just combined, then fold in the apple sauce, orange zest, carrots and chopped nuts. Spoon into the prepared tin and bake for 50 minutes to an hour, until a toothpick inserted into the middle comes out clean. Cool in the tin for 10 minutes before turning out the cake to cool completely on a wire rack.

To prepare the icing, beat the butter until fluffy, then gradually beat in the cream cheese until you have a smooth mixture with no lumps. Beat in the lemon juice and zest. Gradually beat in the icing sugar.

When the cake is completely cold, ice and decorate with the remaining whole nuts.

The cake will keep in an airtight tin, uniced for 3–4 days. It's best iced just before you intend it to be eaten.

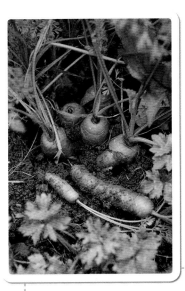

gRowInG CARRoTS

Carrots love light, sandy soil with a fine, crumbly texture so they can develop into nice, straight roots. Sow the seeds directly in the soil from spring through to early summer. Early sowings may need some protection with cloches or horticultural fleece. Successive plantings every few weeks will give you a continuous supply. Sow where you want them to grow as thinning can release chemicals which attract hungry carrot flies. You can deter them by planting some chives (page 23) nearby. Sow carrot seeds very thinly – if you find this difficult, mix the tiny seeds with some sharp sand to make them easier to handle – and cover with a fine layer of soil. Aim to plant them about 1cm deep in rows 12cm apart. Don't let the soil dry out and keep the patch well weeded. Your first carrots should be ready to lift about 8 weeks later.

Hazelnut praline

Clear as amber glass and studded with toasted hazelnuts, this praline is heavenly to nibble on or, chopped or crushed into small pieces, as a delicious decoration for ice cream or cakes. Makes 1 sheet of praline.

GROWING HAZELNUTS

'Hazel' is the common name for a species of nut-bearing shrub which includes the cobnut, *Corylus avellana*, and the filbert, *C. maxima*. Though hazels are theoretically self-fertile, bearing golden male catkins and small, red female flowers on the same bush, often their flowering times don't overlap. As they're wind-pollinated, unless you live in the countryside where there are many wild hazels, you need to plant a mixture of varieties to ensure a good crop. Hazels grow best in well-drained soil in a sunny position, but they will also tolerate a little shade. Young bushes and trees should start to be productive after three or four years – the nuts are ready to harvest when the husks begin to turn yellow in autumn.

150g whole unblanched hazelnuts
150g granulated sugar
½ teaspoon sea salt flakes (optional)
A little vegetable oil, for greasing

30 x 30cm baking tray
Silpat mat (optional)

Preheat the oven to 200°C/gas mark 6. Place the hazelnuts on a high-sided baking sheet and bake until they are fragrant and the skins are blistered, about 5 minutes. Wrap them in a clean tea towel and leave for 5 minutes before rubbing vigorously to remove the skins – don't worry too much if some of the skins remain on the nuts.

Next, make the praline. Assemble everything before you start. Lightly oil the baking tray or line it with a Silpat mat if you have one.

Tip the sugar into a heavy-bottomed saucepan or frying pan. It's better to use a pan which has a pale interior, rather than a dark one, in order to monitor the colour of the caramel more easily. Warm the sugar over a medium heat. It will begin to melt. At this stage, stir it slightly to encourage it to melt evenly. Lower the heat a little and leave to melt completely without stirring until the caramel is a rich, golden brown. Don't leave it unattended even for a moment; it can burn very quickly. As soon as it's ready, tip in the hazelnuts and turn out onto the prepared baking tray, swirling to ensure it's a thin, even layer. Sprinkle over the sea salt, if using. Leave to set and cool for an hour or so before breaking into pieces.

The praline will keep, sealed in an airtight container, for 2 weeks.

PACKAGING Praline makes a great gift for an ice-cream fiend. Seal in a pretty, airtight container alongside an ice-cream scoop and some sundae glasses.

SUPPLIERS

G BALDWIN & CO

London's oldest herbalist, established in 1844. The shop is a fantastic source of many of the materials used in this book, including beeswax, benzoin tincture, liquid Castile soap, dried herbs and flowers, essential oils, oils, orris root and soap-making supplies. Available from the store or online.

G. Baldwin & Co
171/173 Walworth Road
London SE17 1RW
020 7703 5550
www.baldwins.co.uk

BEDWYN STAMPS

Peter Wilmot sells acid-free glassine envelopes in small batches, particularly useful when most online suppliers only sell them by the thousand. Perfect for storing seeds and dried flowers, and for a wide range of other craft projects.
www.bedwynstamps.com

BLACKMOOR NURSERIES

Specialist fruit nursery established by Lord Wolmer in the 1920s. Excellent source of high-quality fruit trees and soft fruit bushes by mail order. See their website for annual open days.

Blackmoor Nurseries
Nr Liss
Hampshire GU33 6BS
01420 477978
www.blackmoor.co.uk

BLOMS BULBS

The Blom family have been cultivating bulbs for over 150 years, and Paul Blom continues that tradition today. Hundreds of varieties of perennial plants and bulbs available mail order, including violas, pinks, lily of the valley, 'Tête-à-Tête', narcissi and grape hyacinths.

Bloms Bulbs, Primrose Nurseries
Melchbourne
Bedfordshire MK44 1ZZ
01234 709099
www.blomsbulbs.com

COLUMBIA ROAD FLOWER MARKET

Sunday street market selling plants, cut flowers and gardening supplies. Particularly worth visiting are the herb stall run by Mick and Sylvia Grover, for a wide range of aromatic, culinary and medicinal herbs, and their son Carl's neighbouring stall for seasonal cut flowers of excellent quality. Also, Red Mud Hut, 92 Columbia Road, for planters and troughs in a wide range of materials. The market is open every Sunday, from 8am until 2.30pm.

Columbia Road
London E2 7RG
www.columbiaroad.info

DAVID AUSTIN ROSES

The Austin family have been growing, breeding and selling roses since 1969. An inspiring source of bare-rooted and container-grown roses by mail order. If you're in Shropshire, do visit their plant centre and 2-acre rose garden which contains over 700 rose varieties.

David Austin Roses Ltd
Bowling Green Lane
Albrighton
Wolverhampton WV7 3HB
01902 376300
www.davidaustinroses.com

DOWNDERRY NURSERY

Home to the Scientific National Plant Collection of Lavender. Sells a dazzling selection of lavenders by mail order, as well as some interesting varieties of rosemary. Open to the public May to October; check website for opening times.

Downderry Nursery
Pillar Box Lane
Hadlow
Tonbridge
Kent TN11 9SW
01732 810081
www.downderry-nursery.co.uk

FIBREX

Founded by Hazel and Dick Key almost 50 years ago and still run by the Key family, Fibrex is the home to the National Pelargonium Collection and the National Hedera (ivies) Collection. Excellent selection of scented pelargoniums available by mail order. The nursery is open to the public; see website for details.

Fibrex Nursery Ltd
Honeybourne Road
Pebworth
Stratford-upon-Avon
Warwickshire CV37 8XP
01789 720788
www.fibrex.co.uk

JEKKA'S HERB FARM

Award-winning organic herb nursery, selling over 650 varieties of culinary, aromatic, decorative and medicinal herbs. Seeds available by mail order, plants from the farm on open days. See website for details.

Jekka's Herb Farm
Rose Cottage
Shellards Lane
Alveston
Bristol BS35 3SY
01454 418878
www.jekkasherbfarm.com

LAKELAND

Award-winning company run by the Rayner family, supplying extensive selection of home and garden products. Great mail-order source for jam pans, jars, jar covers, bottles, labels. See website for store locations.

Lakeland
Alexandra Buildings
Windermere
Cumbria LA23 1BQ
015394 88100
www.lakeland.co.uk

OTTER FARM

Organic Devon smallholding run by Mark Diacono, former head gardener at River Cottage. Carefully chosen selection of unusual vegetable, herb and edible flower seeds. Fruit bushes and trees, including several dwarfing varieties suitable for small gardens and container growing.
www.otterfarm.co.uk

RAINBOW FLORIST SUPPLIES

Online source of garden twine, paper-covered wire, ribbons, wire wreath forms, bags of pine cones and other florists' supplies.
0800 212 869
www.rainbowfloristsupplies.co.uk

SARAH RAVEN

Sarah Raven's very personal selection of bulbs, seeds and plants cultivated at Perch Hill Farm, East Sussex. Great mail order source for cornflowers, dahlias, marigolds and pinks. Also stocks jars and bottles for preserves. Growing, cooking and floristry courses, see website for details.

Sarah Raven's Kitchen & Garden
1 Woodstock Court
Blenheim Road
Marlborough SN8 4AN
0845 092 0283
www.sarahraven.com

SILICASEC

Very efficient mail order source of silica gel, used for drying herbs and flowers.
www.silicasec.co.uk

WOOTENS OF WENHASTON

Excellent mail-order source of perennials. Particularly interesting range of irises and scented pelargoniums. Nursery is open to the public; see website for details.

Wootens of Wenhaston
Halesworth
Suffolk IP19 9HD
01502 478 258
www.wootensplants.com

4CANDLES.CO.UK

Extensive selection of candle-making supplies, including wax, wicks, dye, moulds and double boilers.
www.4candles.co.uk
01482 345414

INDEX